European Yearbook of International Economic Law

Special Issue

The European Yearbook of International Economic Law (EYIEL) is an annual publication in International Economic Law, a field increasingly emancipating itself from Public International Law scholarship and evolving into a fully-fledged academic discipline in its own right. With the yearbook, the editors and publisher intend to make a significant contribution to the development of this "new" discipline and provide an international reference source of the highest possible quality. The EYIEL covers all areas of IEL, in particular WTO Law, External Trade Law for major trading countries, important Regional Economic Integration agreements, International Competition Law, International Investment Regulation, International Monetary Law, International Intellectual Property Protection and International Tax Law. In addition to the regular annual volumes, EYIEL Special Issues routinely address specific current topics in International Economic Law.

More information about this subseries at http://www.springer.com/series/8848

Gabrielle Kaufmann-Kohler • Michele Potestà

Investor-State Dispute Settlement and National Courts

Current Framework and Reform Options

Springer Open

Gabrielle Kaufmann-Kohler
Center for International Dispute Settlement (CIDS)
University of Geneva
Geneva, Switzerland

Michele Potestà
Center for International Dispute Settlement (CIDS), Graduate Institute for International and Development Studies
University of Geneva
Geneva, Switzerland

ISSN 2364-8392 ISSN 2364-8406 (electronic)
European Yearbook of International Economic Law
ISSN 2510-6880 ISSN 2510-6899 (electronic)
Special Issue
ISBN 978-3-030-44163-0 ISBN 978-3-030-44164-7 (eBook)
https://doi.org/10.1007/978-3-030-44164-7

This book is an open access publication.

This Springer imprint is published by the registered company Springer Nature Switzerland AG.
The registered company address is: Gewerbestrasse 11, 6330 Cham, Switzerland

Executive Summary

This study was commissioned by the Swiss Confederation's State Secretariat for Economic Affairs (SECO) to the Geneva Center for International Dispute Settlement (CIDS). Its objective is to examine the multiple intersections between national and international courts in the field of investment protection and to suggest possible modes for regulating jurisdictional interactions between domestic courts and international tribunals going forward. The study seeks to contribute not only to the legal analysis but also to the policy reflections that are necessarily linked to the ongoing initiatives for the reform of investor-State dispute settlement.

The current system of foreign investment protection consists of more than 3000 international investment agreements (IIAs), most of which provide for investment arbitration as the forum for the resolution of disputes between foreign investors and host States. However, national courts also have jurisdiction over certain matters involving cross-border investments. International investment tribunals and national courts thus interact in a number of ways, which vary from harmonious coexistence to reinforcing complementation, reciprocal supervision, and, occasionally, competition and tension. The study maps this complex relationship between dispute settlement bodies in the existing investment treaty context and examines the possible role of domestic courts in future treaty framework(s) which may emerge from the States' current efforts to reform the system.

The study starts by reviewing the existing criticism of investor-State dispute settlement in relation to the role of domestic courts. In essence, this criticism contends that the IIA investment arbitration regime does not account for situations in which domestic courts offer adequate access to justice and discriminates against domestic investors by granting only (certain) foreign investors a privileged procedural track (2.1). In order to place such criticism in a broader context, the study provides an overview of the historical, economic, and political reasons that underpin the creation of the current investment dispute settlement system (2.2) and discusses whether these motivations still justify the existence of an international system of investment dispute resolution, whether in the form of arbitration or standing adjudicatory bodies (2.3).

Chapter 3 surveys how the inter-relationship between domestic courts and investor-State arbitration plays out in the current investment treaty framework. It first looks at the allocation of jurisdiction over investment disputes between courts and arbitral tribunals. Because multiple fora, national and international, may be empowered to adjudicate what in substance is one and the same dispute, jurisdictional overlaps are bound to occur and have indeed become more frequent (3.1). In order to coordinate national and international proceedings, States have devised several models in their IIAs, which respond to different needs and policies. The diverse solutions contained in IIAs include rules on exhaustion of local remedies, domestic litigation requirements short of exhaustion, fork-in-the-road clauses, and waiver provisions. Despite their potential to address jurisdictional overlaps, these clauses could be improved in order to better capture certain undesirable consequences arising from duplicative proceedings in national and international fora (3.2). Significant interactions between domestic courts and international tribunals occur also when courts exercise supervisory functions over investment arbitration proceedings, in particular at annulment and enforcement. In Switzerland, that role has seen a growth in the recent years as a result of the increase of non-ICSID investment arbitration seated in Switzerland, a trend that is likely to continue in the future (3.3). In a further facet of the interplay, investor-State tribunals scrutinize the decisions of domestic courts when faced with a claim alleging court misconduct (3.4).

Finally, Chap. 4 of the study analyzes the possible role which national courts could play in the main reform scenarios which States are currently considering, i.e., if investment arbitration is (i) reformed through targeted adjustments, (ii) supplemented with an appellate mechanism, (iii) replaced by a multilateral investment court, or (iv) supplanted by inter-State mechanisms. Each of these reform scenarios raises specific challenges when it comes to their articulation with domestic courts.

The study concludes that in certain areas of interactions between domestic courts and international investment tribunals, the "division of labor" between the two types of dispute settlement bodies is not always optimal, with the result that inefficiencies burden the system. In these areas, there is a need for improvement by providing for a more fruitful allocation of tasks among domestic and international courts and tribunals, whatever form the latter may take.

Contents

Abbreviations

AM	Appeal mechanism
BIT	Bilateral investment treaty
CETA	Comprehensive Economic and Trade Agreement between the EU and Canada
CIDS Supplemental Report	Gabrielle Kaufmann-Kohler and Michele Potestà, "The Composition of a Multilateral Investment Court and of an Appeal Mechanism for Investment Awards," CIDS Supplemental Report, 15 November 2017
CJEU	Court of Justice of the European Union
ECHR	European Convention on Human Rights
ECT	Energy Charter Treaty
ECtHR	European Court of Human Rights
First CIDS Report	Gabrielle Kaufmann-Kohler and Michele Potestà, "Can the Mauritius Convention serve as a model for the reform of investor-State arbitration in connection with the introduction of a permanent investment tribunal or an appeal mechanism? Analysis and roadmap," CIDS Report, 3 June 2016
FTA	Free trade agreement
ICC	International Chamber of Commerce
ICJ	International Court of Justice
ICSID AF	International Centre for Settlement of Investment Disputes Additional Facility
ICSID Convention	Convention on the Settlement of Investment Disputes between States and Nationals of Other States, 18 March 1965, 575 UNTS 159
ICSID	International Centre for Settlement of Investment Disputes
IIA	International investment agreement
MIC	Multilateral investment court

NAFTA	North American Free Trade Agreement, 17 December 1992, 32 ILM 289, 605 (1993)
NYC	1958 New York Convention on the Recognition and Enforcement of Foreign Arbitral Awards
PCA	Permanent Court of Arbitration
PILA	Swiss Federal Private International Law Act
SCC	Stockholm Chamber of Commerce
SSDS	State-to-State dispute settlement
TTIP	Transatlantic Trade and Investment Partnership
UNCITRAL WGIII	UNCITRAL Working Group III
UNCITRAL	United Nations Commission on International Trade Law
UNCTAD	United Nations Conference on Trade and Development
USMCA	United States–Mexico–Canada Agreement
VCLT	Vienna Convention on the Law of Treaties

Chapter 1
Scope and Objective of This Study

This study was commissioned by the Swiss Confederation's State Secretariat for Economic Affairs (SECO) to the Geneva Center for International Dispute Settlement (CIDS). Its objective is to examine the interactions between national courts and international tribunals in the area of investment law. While most international investment agreements (IIAs)[1] currently provide for investment arbitration as the forum for the resolution of disputes between foreign investors and host States, national courts[2] also have jurisdiction over certain matters involving cross-border investments. This study seeks to map the relationship between national courts and international investment tribunals in the existing IIA context and examine the possible role of domestic courts in future treaty framework(s) which may emerge from the States' current efforts to reform the system. **1.**

As a result of the growing criticisms over, and demands for reform of, investor-State arbitration by States, international organizations, and civil society, over the past years, States have embarked on a significant process of reflection on the existing investment treaty system and, in particular, the investor-State arbitral mechanism **2.**

The authors of this study thank Anna Korshunova, CIDS researcher, for research assistance; Cara North and Christos Stamatis, CIDS researchers, for assistance in finalizing the footnotes; and Erika Hasler, Tabea Seedoch, and Mathew Yarden of the Library Team at Lévy Kaufmann-Kohler for continuous support in locating bibliographic resources. The study is current as of December 2019.

[1]The abbreviation "IIA(s)" is used throughout this study to refer to bilateral investment treaties (BITs), bilateral or regional free trade agreements (FTAs) that include foreign investment obligations (typically contained in a standalone chapter), such as the North American Free Trade Agreement (NAFTA), and sectoral treaties, such as the Energy Charter Treaty (ECT), that include investment obligations. The expression "investment treaties" is sometimes used in this book as synonymous to IIAs.

[2]In relation to courts, this study uses the terms "national", "domestic", "local", and "municipal" as synonymous.

G. Kaufmann-Kohler, M. Potestà, *Investor-State Dispute Settlement and National Courts*, European Yearbook of International Economic Law,
https://doi.org/10.1007/978-3-030-44164-7_1

included in IIAs. In July 2017, the debate concerning investment arbitration reached another level when Member States of the United Nations Commission on International Trade Law (UNCITRAL), including Switzerland, entrusted Working Group III (WGIII) with a "broad mandate to work on the possible reform of investor-State dispute settlement".[3]

3. As can be observed from the discussions that have taken place in WGIII so far, the criticism over investor-State arbitration has multiple facets and dimensions, which range from the perceived length and costs of investment arbitration proceedings, the structural inadequacy of *ad hoc* adjudicatory bodies to ensure consistency in the interpretation of legal issues, to the perceived lack of independence and impartiality of the adjudicators, among others.[4] One of the more fundamental criticisms often voiced against investment arbitration, including in the political discourse, is that national courts are well placed to resolve investment disputes and there is thus no need for foreign investors to be provided with direct access to *international* tribunals for the settlement of such disputes. Other criticisms go to the possible scope of investment arbitration tribunals' powers and the coordination of their actions with that of national courts. These criticisms raise questions that go to the very justification for current or future dispute settlement regimes. Answering these more fundamental questions may be helpful before the more specific concerns identified with the investment treaty regime are addressed in the ongoing reform efforts. A proper understanding of the role of domestic remedies may also be generally useful if and when States move to design new international dispute settlement frameworks, as the question of their interaction with domestic remedies is also likely to arise.

4. Against that background, this study seeks to carry out an in-depth review of the interactions between national courts and international mechanisms for the settlement of investment disputes, in the various forms in which they can be conceived, which includes not only investment arbitration but also standing adjudicatory bodies, such as an appeal mechanism (AM) and a multilateral investment court (MIC). By presenting a comprehensive overview of the many interactions between investor-State dispute settlement and national courts, while at the same time analyzing the possible role which domestic courts may play in the reform scenarios that States and regional organizations are currently considering, this study seeks to add value not

---

[3]See United Nations General Assembly, Report of the United Nations Commission on International Trade Law (Fiftieth Session (3–21 July 2017)), Official Records of the Seventy-second Session, Supplement No. 17 (A/72/17), paras. 263–264.

[4]See for instance, in the UNCITRAL WGIII context, the following UNCITRAL Secretariat papers: *Possible reform of investor-State dispute settlement (ISDS) - Note by the Secretariat*, A/CN.9/WG.III/WP.149; *Possible reform of investor-State dispute settlement (ISDS) Consistency and related matters - Note by the Secretariat*, A/CN.9/WG.III/WP.150; *Possible reform of investor-State dispute settlement (ISDS) Ensuring independence and impartiality on the part of arbitrators and decision makers in ISDS - Note by the Secretariat*, A/CN.9/WG.III/WP.151; *Possible reform of investor-State dispute settlement (ISDS) Arbitrators and decision makers: appointment mechanisms and related issues - Note by the Secretariat*, A/CN.9/WG.III/WP.152; *Possible reform of investor-State dispute settlement (ISDS) Cost and duration - Note by the Secretariat*, A/CN.9/WG.III/WP.153.

only to the legal analysis, but also to the policy reflections that are necessarily linked to the ongoing reform initiatives. It is also meant to promote a better understanding of the multiple intersections that exist and are likely to continue to exist between national and international courts in the field of investment protection, and to suggest possible modes for regulating jurisdictional interactions going forward.

The study is organized as follows. After these introductory remarks, Chap. 2 reviews the existing criticism of investor-State dispute settlement *in relation to the role of domestic courts* (*infra* at 2.1). Understanding this criticism requires consideration of the historical, economic, and political reasons that underpin the creation of the current investment dispute settlement system (*infra* at 2.2) and assessing whether those reasons remain valid in today's world (*infra* at 2.3). Chapter 3 examines the multiple and often complex ways in which the two systems—national judiciary and international tribunals—interact in the *existing* IIA framework. Chapter 4 then moves to the main reform scenarios which States are currently considering, with a view to analyzing the possible role which national courts could play if investment arbitration is (i) reformed through targeted adjustments, (ii) supplemented with an AM, (iii) replaced with a MIC, or (iv) supplanted by inter-State mechanisms. It will also take account of the scenario where investment arbitration is entirely eliminated without being replaced by an alternative international mechanism, which would result in a system where domestic proceedings operate as the sole forum for the settlement of investment disputes. Chapter 5 sets out the conclusions and recommendations in light of the analysis carried out in the previous sections. **5.**

The main points of intersection between domestic courts and international investment tribunals examined in this study touch on issues of jurisdiction, admissibility, merits, and procedure. The questions examined thus cut across almost the entirety of the law of investment protection in both its substantive and procedural aspects, and have given rise to difficulties in their application and often splits in the jurisprudence. Given the breadth of the issues, the study's approach is to focus primarily on State practice as reflected in the conclusion of IIAs and the policy choices underlying the treaty texts. In so doing, it does not limit the examination to IIAs of certain countries or regions, but seeks to provide a global picture of the IIA practice worldwide to the extent relevant to the issue discussed. **6.**

This being said, the study devotes special attention to Swiss practice. Switzerland is a party to the ICSID Convention and has concluded over 110 BITs with its trade partners, making it one of the economies with the widest IIA network worldwide.[5] Swiss BITs have been invoked in at least 20 known investor-State disputes by Swiss **7.**

[5]See SECO, "Overview of BITs – List of BITs concluded by Switzerland - May 21st 2019", available at https://www.seco.admin.ch/seco/en/home/Aussenwirtschaftspolitik_Wirtschaftliche_Zusammenarbeit/Wirtschaftsbeziehungen/Internationale_Investitionen/Vertragspolitik_der_Schweiz/overview-of-bits.html, listing the BITs concluded by Switzerland. See also UNCTAD, International Investment Agreements Navigator, "Switzerland", available at https://investmentpolicy.unctad.org/international-investment-agreements/countries/203/switzerland. On Switzerland's BIT practice, see generally Schmid (2013), pp. 651–696.

investors.[6] Furthermore, Switzerland has been traditionally one of the most chosen seats for international arbitration, including (non-ICSID) investment arbitrations, due to, *inter alia*, the country's reputation for neutrality and stability as well as the legislation's and the judiciary's pro-arbitration approach. In the last few years, there has been an increase in Swiss-seated investment treaty arbitrations, a trend which may well continue especially for intra-EU disputes as a result of the uncertainties arising from the judgment by the Court of Justice of the European Union (CJEU) in *Achmea*.[7] An increase of Swiss-seated arbitrations means, in turn, a potentially greater involvement of the Swiss Federal Tribunal with investment matters.[8]

8. Before embarking on the analysis, a point of terminology is in order. The authors of this study are of the view that the term "ISDS" (which is the acronym for "investor-State dispute settlement" and which is often employed in the reform discussions) is imprecise and may have different meanings depending on the context in which it is used. In its colloquial and perhaps most widely used meaning, the term is essentially synonymous with the current investor-State *international arbitration* system.[9] Yet, the a-technical formula "investor-State dispute settlement" does not, in its plain meaning, exclude a possibly broader range of dispute settlement mechanisms. First, there is no semantic reason why it could not encompass non-binding methods of dispute settlement between investors and States, such as conciliation, mediation, ombudsman, and so on. Second, even if one were to limit the scope of the term to *binding* means of dispute resolution, "ISDS" could well encompass settlement methods beyond the current arbitral system, for instance the MIC. In other words, the current use of the term "ISDS" does not make clear what is the defining characteristic of "ISDS" vis-à-vis "other" mechanisms. Is it the investor's standing to bring a claim *in its own name* against the State (if so, ISDS would include investment arbitration, with or without an AM, MIC, and domestic courts)? Or is it the fact that the dispute resolution method is *international* as opposed to national? Or is it a combination of both criteria, such that only means of dispute resolution that offer investors *direct* access to an *international* forum qualify as ISDS?

9. Absent clarity as to the contours of what constitutes ISDS (and what does not), and in light of the fact that the ongoing reform discussions as well as the present study seek to reflect upon several distinct dispute settlement mechanisms beyond investment arbitration, for the sake of clarity this study will avoid employing the

---

[6] See Scherer and Murphy (2019), pp. 9–26. By contrast, Switzerland has never been a respondent in an investor-State dispute under an IIA. In April 2014, consultations between a foreign investor and Switzerland were commenced under an IIA. However, no arbitration appears to have been started. See Jarrod Hepburn (2015), *Uzan family may return to ICSID, as Switzerland reveals details of threatened investor claim*, IAReporter, 17 March 2015.

[7] See CJEU C-284/16, *Slovak Republic v. Achmea BV*, 6 March 2018.

[8] See *infra* at 3.3.

[9] This is also the meaning that appears to be given in the UNCITRAL Secretariat papers. See, e.g., UNCITRAL Working Group III, *Possible reform of investor-State dispute settlement (ISDS)* - Note by the Secretariat, A/CN.9/WG.III/WP.142, paras. 5–7 (describing the "characteristics of the ISDS regime").

term "ISDS" to the extent possible. It will instead refer to the different (binding) methods of investment dispute resolution on the international plane using the following terms, which in the authors' view capture more precisely their defining characteristics:

- "investor-State arbitration" (or "investment arbitration") is used to refer to a dispute resolution mechanism which allows a foreign investor to bring a claim in its own name against the host State before an adjudicatory body in the nature of an arbitral tribunal, for instance ICSID or UNCITRAL arbitration. Although investor-State arbitration may be based on a contract or a domestic law on foreign investment, this study is primarily concerned with arbitrations based on IIAs, i.e. "investment treaty arbitrations";
- "investment arbitration with an AM" (or similar formulations) is used to refer to the traditional *arbitration* mechanism supplemented with a review mechanism in the form of a standing appellate mechanism[10];
- "multilateral investment court" or "MIC" is used to refer to a permanent multilateral adjudicatory body for the resolution of investment disputes, in which foreign investors would have standing to bring claims in their own name against host States[11];
- "State-to-State dispute settlement" (or "SSDS") is used to refer to inter-State mechanisms, routinely included in IIAs and typically in the form of arbitration, for the resolution of disputes on the interpretation and/or application of IIAs.

References

Scherer M, Murphy L (2019) Inventory of arbitration proceedings based on Swiss bilateral investment treaties (BIT) (Update 2018). ASA Bull 37(1):9–26

Schmid M (2013) Switzerland. In: Brown C (ed) Commentaries on selected model investment treaties. Oxford University Press, pp 651–696

---

[10] An appellate mechanism complementing investor-State arbitration could be bilateral or multilateral. See, for instance, Article 9.23 of the China-Australia FTA (2015), which provides that within 3 years after its date of entry into force the parties to the FTA shall commence negotiations with a view to establishing a bilateral appellate mechanism to review awards on questions of law. For an example of a "*rendez-vous*" clause concerning a multilateral appellate mechanism, see for instance, U.S. Model BIT (2004), Article 28, para. 10 and Australia-Republic of Korea FTA (2014), Article 11.2, para. 13 and Annex 11-E.

[11] A MIC could be with or without a built-in appellate mechanism. See Gabrielle Kaufmann-Kohler and Michele Potestà (2016), *Can the Mauritius Convention serve as a model for the reform of investor-State arbitration in connection with the introduction of a permanent investment tribunal or an appeal mechanism? Analysis and Roadmap,* CIDS Report (hereinafter "Gabrielle Kaufmann-Kohler and Michele Potestà (2016), *First CIDS Report*"), Section V.D.

Chapter 2
Why Investment Arbitration and Not Domestic Courts? The Origins of the Modern Investment Dispute Resolution System, Criticism, and Future Outlook

This Chapter first summarizes the criticism voiced against investment treaty arbitration *with specific regard to its relationship with domestic courts* (*infra* at Sect. 2.1). It does not seek to discuss all of the multiple concerns raised against investment arbitration, which have already been addressed in the authors' First CIDS Report[1] and are further examined in the UNCITRAL Secretariat's papers,[2] among other materials.[3] Discussing the criticism of investment arbitration vis-à-vis domestic courts requires providing an overview of the main reasons why States created the investment treaty system in the first place (*infra* at Sect. 2.2) and examining today's justifications for keeping or putting in place an international system of investment dispute resolution, whether in the form of arbitration or standing adjudicatory bodies (*infra* at Sect. 2.3). The following sub-sections will in particular ask: What goals were IIAs intended to achieve? In light of those goals, what is the function of international courts and tribunals in the investment law domain, either in their current arbitral configuration or in future constellations such as a MIC? As States are considering questions concerning the institutional design and re-design of the system, it appears important to seek to provide answers to these questions in order to test the continuing validity of the assumptions which underpin the conclusion of investment treaties with international dispute resolution mechanisms. **10.**

[1] See Gabrielle Kaufmann-Kohler and Michele Potestà (2016), *First CIDS Report*, paras. 18–23.

[2] See, *inter alia*, the UNCITRAL Secretariat papers cited *supra* at Chap. 1, footnote 4. See also *Possible reform of investor-State dispute settlement (ISDS): Third-party funding - Note by the Secretariat*, A/CN.9/WG.III/WP.157.

[3] See the "Bibliography of writings relating to ISDS reform" prepared by the CIDS available at https://www.cids.ch/academic-forum.

G. Kaufmann-Kohler, M. Potestà, *Investor-State Dispute Settlement and National Courts*, European Yearbook of International Economic Law,
https://doi.org/10.1007/978-3-030-44164-7_2

2.1 Criticism Over Investment Treaty Arbitration in Relation to Domestic Courts

11. In recent years, a number of States, academics, and members of civil society have increasingly questioned the justification for maintaining in place a dispute resolution system which allows foreign investors to bring direct claims against sovereign States before international arbitral tribunals rather than before the courts of the host State.

12. Looking at the big picture, there are essentially two inter-related criticisms against investment treaty arbitration vis-à-vis domestic courts. First, it is argued that there is no need to put or maintain in place an international system for the resolution of investment disputes because investors in any event "retain rights under domestic systems" and those systems "are often assumed, but not established, to be inadequate".[4] In other words, the current IIA investment arbitration regime does not account for situations in which domestic courts *do* offer adequate access to justice to a foreign investor.[5] In a similar vein, critics contend that the IIA framework allows investors to bring claims against sovereigns without having to exhaust local remedies in the host State, regardless of whether those remedies are capable of delivering justice.[6] In fact, IIAs generally remove the duty to exhaust local remedies even for countries that have mature and advanced legal systems.[7]

13. Secondly, critics underscore that the procedural right to resort to arbitration against the host State under an IIA is not available to domestic investors (and foreign investors of nationalities not covered by IIAs). If domestic remedies are assumed to be unreliable, why allow only (certain) foreign investors to benefit from an international adjudicative process? In the eyes of those making this criticism, such differential treatment is seen as unfair and illustrative of "the privileges accorded by less developed countries to multilateral corporations at the expense of local investors who are competitively disadvantaged".[8]

14. A number of States, including capital-exporters and traditional supporters of the investment treaty system, have recently invoked principles of primacy of domestic courts over international tribunals and of non-discrimination between local and foreign investors in justification of anti-investment arbitration policies. The idea that foreign investors should enjoy no greater rights than domestic investors, including procedural rights,[9] has been put forward by a range of actors, such as the

---

[4]Lise Johnson, Lisa Sachs, Brooke Güven, and Jesse Coleman (2018), *Clearing the Path: Withdrawal of Consent and Termination as Next Steps for Reforming International Investment Law*, Columbia Center on Sustainable Development Policy Paper, April 2018, p. 10.

[5]Van Harten (2010), p. 34.

[6]Van Harten (2010), p. 35.

[7]Van Harten (2010), p. 35.

[8]Trackman (2012), p. 994 (discussing the criticism).

[9]Whether IIAs grant greater *substantive* rights than those provided under the relevant domestic systems of States entering into those IIAs is controversial and it likely depends on the laws of the relevant State. With regard to U.S. IIAs, Parvanov and Kantor conclude that U.S. IIAs generally do

Australian Government, the European Parliament, and the U.S. Administration under President Trump, among others.[10] In 2011, for instance, the Australian Government headed by Prime Minister Gillard openly indicated that it would no longer agree to investment arbitration in its treaties based, *inter alia*, on reasons of equal treatment between foreign and domestic investors.[11] In its 2015 recommendations to the European Commission on the negotiations of the Transatlantic Trade and Investment Partnership (TTIP), the European Parliament called on the Commission "to ensure that foreign investors are treated in a non-discriminatory fashion and have a fair opportunity to seek and achieve redress of grievances, while benefiting from no greater rights than domestic investors, and to oppose the inclusion of ISDS

---

not confer greater substantive rights on foreign investors than the protection afforded to domestic investors under comparable U.S. domestic law (Parvanov and Kantor 2012, pp. 741–836); Johnson and Volkov come to an opposite conclusion and argue that fair and equitable treatment provisions in BITs are more favorable to foreign investors than U.S. law (Johnson and Volkov 2013, pp. 361–415). With respect to EU law, Kleinheisterkamp also finds that investment treaties provide more generous rights than EU law (Kleinheisterkamp 2012, pp. 85–109). Bonnitcha, Poulsen, and Waibel note that these debates are particularly controversial because both the U.S. Congress and the European Parliament have issued directives to their countries' treaty negotiators stating that investment treaties should not provide greater substantive rights than are available under their respective national laws (see *infra* in the text, para. 14). However, they are of the view that "because relatively little research has been done comparing the substantive rights in investment treaties with those available under domestic law, it is unclear whether the directives are being followed in practice." See Bonnitcha et al. (2017), p. 153. With regard to *procedural* rights, it is undisputed that the investor-State arbitration mechanism is not offered as a remedy under domestic law.

[10]See also South African Department of Trade and Industry, Government Position Paper on *Bilateral Investment Treaty Policy Framework Review* (Pretoria, June 2009), p. 45 (noting that "[t]here is no compelling reason why review of an investor's claims against a state cannot be undertaken by the institutions of the state in question—provided these are independent of the public authority that is in dispute and they discharge their duties in accordance with basic principles of good governance, including an independent judiciary. Unfortunately, there is little indication in the texts of BITs that negotiators have acted with prudence to promote better domestic dispute settlement in the host state").

[11]See Australian Government (Department of Foreign Affairs and Trade), *Gillard Government Trade Policy Statement: Trading our way to more jobs and prosperity* (April 2011), p. 14 (stating that "[t]he Gillard Government supports the principle of national treatment – that foreign and domestic businesses are treated equally under the law. However, the Government does not support provisions that would confer greater legal rights on foreign businesses than those available to domestic businesses. [...] In the past, Australian Governments have sought the inclusion of investor-state dispute resolution procedures in trade agreements with developing countries at the behest of Australian businesses. The Gillard Government will discontinue this practice. If Australian businesses are concerned about sovereign risk in Australian trading partner countries, they will need to make their own assessments about whether they want to commit to investing in those countries"). Following changes in government, the policy appears to have changed, as now Australia considers inclusion of investor-State arbitration clauses "on a case-by-case basis". See Australian Government (Department of Foreign Affairs and Trade), "Investor-State-Dispute-Settlement (ISDS)", available at https://dfat.gov.au/trade/investment/Pages/investor-state-dispute-settlement.aspx. See also Amokura Kawharu and Luke Nottage (2018), *Renouncing Investor-State Dispute Settlement in Australia, then New Zealand: Déjà vu*, The University of Sydney Law School Legal Studies Research Paper Series No. 18/03 (February 2018), p. 5.

in the TTIP, as other options to enforce investment protection are available, such as domestic remedies".[12] In the context of the recent NAFTA re-negotiations, the U.S. Trade Representative explained to Congress that the U.S. Government was "skeptical about ISDS" *inter alia* because investor-State arbitration grants "a foreign national [. . .] more rights than Americans have in the American court system",[13] and suggested that investors should resort to State-to-State dispute settlement or negotiate arbitration provisions in their contracts as more appropriate alternatives.[14]

15. Although not always expressly articulated in these terms, these positions appear to question the very premise upon which the system was created. Indeed, it is often argued that the reasons why an international forum for the settlement of investment disputes was established included the need to provide (i) a neutral forum as alternative to domestic courts that were perceived as inadequate, and (ii) a substitute to traditional State-to-State "politicized" mechanisms. These reasons are analyzed in the next chapter on the origins of the investor-State arbitration regime, together with

[12]European Parliament (2015) Opinion of the Committee on Legal Affairs for the Committee on International Trade on recommendations to the European Commission on the negotiations for the Transatlantic Trade and Investment Partnership (2014/2228INI), 4 May 2015, Rapporteur Dietmar Köster, p. 4. See also Opinion of the European Committee of the Regions (2015), 110th Plenary Session, 11–13 February 2015, (2015/C 140/02), 28 April 2015, paras. 33–35.

[13]See U.S. Trade Representative Robert Lighthizer at hearing before the U.S. Congress Ways and Means Committee, 21 March 2018 (transcript available on the International Economic Law and Policy Blog at https://worldtradelaw.typepad.com/ielpblog/2018/03/brady-lighthizer-isds-exchange.html and video available at https://www.c-span.org/video/?c4719932/brady-lighthizer-isds-discussion (where U.S. Trade Representative Robert Lighthizer noted that "[w]e are skeptical about ISDS for a variety of reasons [. . .]. Number one, on the U.S. side there are questions of sovereignty. Why should a foreign national be able to come in and not only have the rights of Americans in the American court system but have more rights than Americans have in the American court system? It strikes me as something that at least we ought to be skeptical of and analyze. So a U.S. person goes into a court system, goes through the system and they're stuck with what they get. If a foreign national can do that and then at the end of the day say 'I want three guys in London to say we're going to overrule the entire US system.' [. . .] So this is troubling in that respect"). The renegotiations of the NAFTA resulted in the conclusion of the so-called USMCA which eliminated future investor-State arbitration as between the U.S. and Canada and curtailed its scope as between the U.S. and Mexico. See Galbraith (2019), pp. 150–159.

[14]See U.S. Trade Representative Robert Lighthizer at hearing before the U.S. Congress Ways and Means Committee, 21 March 2018, *supra* Chap. 2, footnote 13 (stating that "[o]ur view was that rather than have this mandatory ISDS provision, which we think is a problem in terms of our sovereignty in the United States, encourages outsourcing and losing jobs in the United States, and by the way lowering standards in a variety of places, that we should be very careful before we put something like that into place. So you say 'What are the risks, what are the alternatives for these companies?' The first alternative I'd say is state-to-state dispute settlement, the second alternative is if you go to any one of these companies and ask them 'Why do you need this; why don't you put in place an arbitration provision in your contract?' They'll all say 'Well we could do that,' and indeed they did do it—did it before we had ISDS. In a country like Mexico they subscribe to all the conventions and they have to enforce those. If they put [an] arbitration provision in their contract, these things are then resolved in a similar manner, but without the United States ceding sovereignty in order to encourage people to outsource jobs. It's just not a good trade in my opinion").

others that were invoked to justify the creation of the investment treaty system (*infra* at Sect. 2.2).

2.2 The Origins of Investor-State Arbitration

This chapter starts by describing the pillars on which the existing investment treaty arbitration framework rests, namely the ICSID Convention and the complex network of IIAs, the majority of which include investor-State arbitration clauses (*infra* at Sect. 2.2.1). It then provides a brief overview of the main reasons that are often put forward for the creation of the investment treaty system (*infra* at Sect. 2.2.2), namely the need to attract foreign investment (*infra* at Sect. 2.2.2.1); the desire to "depoliticize" investment disputes (*infra* at Sect. 2.2.2.2); and the desire to establish a neutral forum on the international plane as an alternative to domestic courts perceived to be inadequate (*infra* at Sect. 2.2.2.3). Bearing the ongoing reform discussions in mind, it then provides an evaluation of whether today's world still needs an international system for the resolution of investment disputes (in the form of arbitration or standing adjudicatory bodies) (*infra* at Sect. 2.3). **16.**

2.2.1 The Pillars of the Investment Treaty Arbitration Framework: The ICSID Convention and the IIAs

The existing investor-State arbitration framework emerged in its modern form in the 1960s, with the conclusion of the ICSID Convention and the first BITs.[15] The investment treaty network has grown since then to comprise more than 3000 IIAs binding a multitude of States worldwide. Switzerland is amongst the 154 Contracting States to the ICSID Convention and has concluded over 110 BITs with its trade partners.[16] Along with Germany, Switzerland was one of the first countries to **17.**

[15]For historical accounts see Newcombe and Paradell (2009), pp. 44–46, para. 1.31; Miles (2013), pp. 86–87. As Newcombe and Paradell explain, "uniqueness of the current IIA network is a product of an historical evolution going as far back as the Middle Ages. Prior to the twentieth century, international standards of foreign investment and investor protection developed primarily through the related processes of diplomatic protection and claims commissions. In the late nineteenth and early twentieth centuries, as the world economy became increasingly internationalized, the limits of the diplomatic protection model became apparent, particularly as controversies arose between capital exporting and importing states regarding the customary international law minimum standard of treatment to be accorded to foreign investors and investments. In the aftermath of the Second World War (WWII), the process of international economic integration was rekindled, leading to the emergence of the contemporary investment treaty framework." (citations omitted) pp. 2–3.

[16]See SECO, "Overview of BITs – List of BITs concluded by Switzerland - May 21st 2019", available at https://www.seco.admin.ch/seco/en/home/Aussenwirtschaftspolitik_Wirtschaftliche_Zusammenarbeit/Wirtschaftsbeziehungen/Internationale_Investitionen/Vertragspolitik_der_

develop a BIT program and is today one of the economies with the widest IIA network worldwide.[17]

18. The ICSID Convention was concluded in 1965 under the aegis of the World Bank and provides for a mechanism for the settlement of investment disputes available to foreign investors and host States in the form of both conciliation and arbitration. More specifically in relation to arbitration,[18] the ICSID Convention allows a Contracting Party and a national of *another* Contracting Party (thus, to the exclusion of domestic investors)[19] to settle their disputes arising out of an investment through arbitration, provided the parties have separately consented to it.[20] The Convention also provides for an effective regime for the enforcement of arbitral awards rendered under the Convention, whereby Contracting Parties undertake to enforce the pecuniary obligations arising out of the award in their territory as if it were a final judgment of their courts.[21]

19. ICSID has administered more than 720 arbitrations to date, most of which in the last two decades.[22] In the majority of cases, the basis for the jurisdiction of the Centre was an IIA incorporating an investor-State arbitration clause. Indeed, from the end of the 1960s,[23] BITs started to include a standing offer from a Contracting Party to submit disputes with the investors of the other Contracting Party to international arbitration, whether ICSID or other arbitral fora, such as UNCITRAL, Stockholm Chamber of Commerce (SCC), or International Chamber of Commerce (ICC). According to UNCTAD, 90% of the existing IIAs contain advance consent (i.e. by

---

Schweiz/overview-of-bits.html, listing the BITs concluded by Switzerland. See also UNCTAD, International Investment Agreements Navigator, "Switzerland", available at https://investmentpolicy.unctad.org/international-investment-agreements/countries/203/switzerland.

[17]See UNCTAD Investment Policy Hub, International Investment Agreements Navigator, "IIAs by Economy", available at https://investmentpolicy.unctad.org/international-investment-agreements/by-economy.

[18]In practice, the conciliation part of the ICSID Convention has had significantly less importance than the arbitration part.

[19]Subject to the rule in Article 25, para. 2(b), second sentence on local companies subject to foreign control.

[20]The Convention is subject to a "dual-consent" requirement, in the sense that "no Contracting State shall by the mere fact of its ratification, acceptance or approval of this Convention and without its consent be deemed to be under any obligation to submit any particular dispute to conciliation or arbitration". See ICSID Convention, Preamble.

[21]See ICSID Convention, Article 54, para. 1.

[22]See ICSID, *The ICSID Caseload – Statistics,* Issue 2019-2, p. 7 available at https://icsid.worldbank.org/en/Documents/ICSID_Web_Stats_2019-2_(English).pdf.

[23]The first BIT to contain an unconditional offer of consent to submit disputes between a Contracting Party and an investor of the other Contracting Party to arbitration is considered to be the Italy-Chad BIT of 1969. See Italy-Chad BIT (1969), Article 7, referring to arbitration under the jurisdiction of the ICSID, pursuant to the Washington Convention of 18 March 1965 (the ICSID Convention). See Newcombe and Paradell (2009), p. 45, para. 1.31.

way of a standing offer) to investment arbitration.[24] In 1990, an ICSID arbitral tribunal recognized for the first time the possibility for an investor to sue a host State on the basis of the offer of consent contained in an IIA,[25] paving the way for the initiation of hundreds of investment treaty claims in the following decades.[26]

2.2.2 *The Reasons for Putting the System in Place*

What were the reasons that prompted States to set up the international treaty framework for the protection of foreign investments, including the grant of direct remedies against host States? Three main reasons are usually advanced for the conclusion of IIAs and, more specifically, for the inclusion of investor-State arbitration therein. First, IIAs, including the grant of direct means of enforcement on the international plane, are said to be aimed at attracting foreign direct investment to host States (*infra* at Sect. 2.2.2.1). Second, investor-State arbitration is said to pursue the objective of "de-politicizing" disputes (*infra* at Sect. 2.2.2.2). Third, and of direct relevance to the subject matter of this study, IIAs provide international remedies directly to foreign investors with a view to affording foreign investors an alternative to domestic courts which are perceived to be inadequate for the resolution of investment disputes (*infra* at Sect. 2.2.2.3). 20.

2.2.2.1 Do Investment Treaties Increase Foreign Investment Flows?

If one looks at the preamble to the ICSID Convention, the very first consideration recorded by States for the conclusion of that Convention is "the need for international cooperation for economic development, and the role of private international investment therein".[27] The Report of the Executive Directors of the International Bank for Reconstruction and Development, or World Bank, which accompanies the 21.

---

[24]According to UNCTAD, 95% of IIAs provide "advance consent to international arbitration". See UNCTAD 2018 World Investment Report, Investment and New Industrial Policies, p. 106 available at https://unctad.org/en/PublicationsLibrary/wir2018_en.pdf.

[25]*Asian Agricultural Products Ltd. v. Republic of Sri Lanka*, Final Award, ICSID Case No. ARB/87/3, Final Award, 27 June 1990, paras. 18–24. See also Pauwelyn (2014), p. 397. A few years before, on 27 November 1985, an ICSID tribunal in its Decision on Preliminary Objections to Jurisdiction had recognized the same possibility under an offer of consent in a domestic law on foreign investment (see *Southern Pacific Properties (Middle East) Limited v. Arab Republic of Egypt*, ICSID Case No. ARB/84/3, Award on the Merits, 20 May 1992, paras. 3, 15).

[26]According to UNCTAD, as of 1 January 2019, "the total number of known ISDS cases pursuant to [IIAs] had reached 942" in the various arbitral fora (see UNCTAD, *Fact Sheet on Investor-State Dispute Settlement Cases in 2018*, IIA Issues Note on International Investment Agreements No 2, May 2019, p. 1).

[27]See ICSID Convention, Preamble.

Convention explains the link between the orderly settlement of investment disputes and the stimulation of private international investments and economic development in the following terms[28]:

> 9. In submitting the attached Convention to governments, the Executive Directors are prompted by the desire to strengthen the partnership between countries in the cause of economic development. The creation of an institution designed to facilitate the settlement of disputes between States and foreign investors can be a major step toward promoting an atmosphere of mutual confidence and thus stimulating a larger flow of private international capital into those countries which wish to attract it. [...]
>
> The Executive Directors believe that private capital will continue to flow to countries offering a favorable climate for attractive and sound investments, even if such countries did not become parties to the Convention or, having joined, did not make use of the facilities of the Centre. On the other hand, *adherence to the Convention by a country would provide additional inducement and stimulate a larger flow of private international investment into its territories, which is the primary purpose of the Convention.*[29]

22. Preambles of IIAs, and of BITs in particular, similarly stress the Contracting States' desire to create favorable conditions for greater investments and often declare that the encouragement and reciprocal protection of investments through an international treaty will be "conducive to the stimulation" of foreign direct investment.[30] Indeed, these objectives are reflected in the headings of many of these treaties, which were traditionally named agreements "on *encouragement* [or promotion] and reciprocal protection of investments".

23. In recent decades, the question of the impact of IIAs on investment flows has been subject to closer scrutiny. Numerous studies have been conducted with a view to assessing the actual effect on foreign direct investments of (i) IIAs generally and (ii) dispute settlement provisions in IIAs more specifically. Those studies have come to diverging conclusions.[31]

---

[28]See Schreuer et al. (2009), p. 4, citing para. 9 of the Report of the Executive Directors on the Convention on the Settlement of Investment Disputes Between States and Nationals of Other States, Section III, 18 March 1965, para. 9.

[29]Report of the Executive Directors on the Convention on the Settlement of Investment Disputes Between States and Nationals of Other States, Section III, 18 March 1965, paras. 9, 12 (emphasis added). For the discussions during the negotiations of the Convention on whether the proposed instrument would increase foreign investment flows or at least improve the "investment climate", see the comprehensive analysis in St John (2018), pp. 154–161.

[30]See, e.g. U.S. Model BIT (2012), Preamble (whereby the Contracting Parties "[*r*]*ecogniz[e]* that agreement on the treatment to be accorded such investment will stimulate the flow of private capital and the economic development of the Parties"); Turkey Model BIT (2009), Preamble ("Recognizing that agreement upon the treatment to be accorded such investment will stimulate the flow of capital and technology and the economic development of the Contracting Parties"); UK Model BIT (2008), Preamble ("Recogni[z]ng that the encouragement and reciprocal protection under international agreement of such investments will be conducive to the stimulation of individual business initiative and will increase prosperity in both States").

[31]See for example Neumayer and Spess (2005), pp. 1582–1583, who find strong evidence that developing countries that sign bilateral investment treaties enjoy significant increases in FDI, as compared to Jennifer Tobin and Susan Rose-Ackerman (2005) (Jennifer Tobin and Susan Rose-

With regard to IIAs in general, according to a 2014 report of the United Nations Conference on Trade and Development (UNCTAD), the majority of the studies reviewed concluded that there was a positive causal relationship between investment treaties and foreign direct investment.[32] A 2017 review by Bonnitcha, Poulsen, and Waibel of the existing quantitative studies on the effect of investment treaties on FDI concludes that "[a] majority find that investment treaties have a positive and statistically significant impact on inward FDI in at least some circumstances", whereas "a sizeable minority of studies find that there is no statistically significant effect of BIT adoption on FDI flows".[33] **24.**

25. The methodological and measurement challenges associated with these empirical studies make it difficult to draw firm conclusions from the existing literature.[34] As remarked in the UNCTAD report, "an empirical correlation [between the presence of IIAs and FDI] does not necessarily imply causation", and "[t]he causal relationship between IIAs and FDI might theoretically run in both directions".[35] Furthermore, some studies observe that the correlation between BITs and the growth in FDI varies according to the States and the BIT models surveyed and hence conclude that any such positive economic result is not necessarily attributable to BITs.[36] Market

---

Ackerman (2005), *Foreign Direct Investment and the Business Environment in Developing Countries: The Impact of Bilateral Investment Treaties*, Yale Law & Economics Research Paper No. 293, 2 May 2005) who find a very weak relationship between BITs and FDI, and Mary Hallward-Driemeier (2003) (Mary Hallward-Driemeier (2003), *Do Bilateral Investment Treaties Attract FDI? Only a bit…and they could bite*, World Bank, Policy Research Paper WPS 3121) who finds no effect of BITs on FDI when looking at bilateral FDI flows from OECD countries to developing countries.

[32]UNCTAD (2014), p. 5.

[33]Bonnitcha et al. (2017), p. 159; see also, pp. 179–180, for the list of surveyed studies.

[34]See in particular Bonnitcha et al. (2017), pp. 155–180. See also Chaisse and Bellak (2015), pp. 79–115; Chaisse and Bellak (2011), pp. 3–10.

[35]UNCTAD (2014), p. 5. In a similar vein, a former U.S. BIT negotiator, Kenneth Vandevelde, suggests that capital-exporting States may prioritize BIT negotiations with trade partners that already were hosts to large amounts of their investments, "so that BITs may be caused by investment flows, rather than the other way around". See Vandevelde (1998), pp. 524–525. See also Swenson (2005), pp. 145–149.

[36]See Jennifer Tobin and Susan Rose-Ackerman (2005), *Foreign Direct Investment and the Business Environment in Developing Countries: The Impact of Bilateral Investment Treaties*, Yale Law & Economics Research Paper No. 293, 2 May 2005, p. 23.

factors and other host country factors,[37] including institutional quality[38] and the level of political risk,[39] may also be determinative for FDI inflows. Other variables, including the specific content of IIAs, e.g. the incorporation of certain substantive provisions, may also determine the effectiveness of BITs in attracting FDI.[40]

26. Surveys carried out with investors and other economic actors aimed at testing their awareness of the investment treaty system and in particular at understanding whether the presence of an IIA affects their investment decisions have also led to mixed results.[41]

27. In addition, a number of studies have specifically focused on the possible effect of investment treaty arbitration provisions on FDI flows.[42] Certain studies have found that there is weak evidence of a relationship between the international dispute settlement provisions included in IIAs and FDI,[43] and that investment treaties that provide advance consent to arbitration are no more effective in attracting FDI than those that do not.[44] In a 2010 report, Australia's Productivity Commission referred to

---

[37]Tobin and Rose-Ackerman (2006), pp. 18–21, discussing, *inter alia*, the impact of entering into a BIT with an OECD country; Allee and Peinhardt (2011), pp. 429–430, discussing the role of facing BIT claims on FDI flows; Tortian (2012), pp. 21–22, discussing, *inter alia*, the market and growth variables for OECD countries' investors. See also Jennifer Tobin and Susan Rose-Ackerman (2005), *Foreign Direct Investment and the Business Environment in Developing Countries: The Impact of Bilateral Investment Treaties*, Yale Law and Economics Research Paper No. 293, 2 May 2005, pp. 1–52, 15, 21; Jason W. Yackee (2006), *Sacrificing Sovereignty: Bilateral Investment Treaties, International Arbitration, and the Quest for Capital*, USC CLEO Research Paper No. C06-15, pp. 2–92, 19–20.

[38]Till Siegmann (2007), *The Impact of Bilateral Investment Treaties and Double Taxation Treaties on Foreign Direct Investments*, University of St. Gallen Law School Law and Economics Research Paper Series, Working Paper No. 2008-22 (November 2007), discussing, *inter alia*, institutional quality.

[39]Jason W. Yackee (2007), *Do BITs Really Work? Revisiting the Empirical Link Between Investment Treaties and Foreign Direct Investment*, Legal Studies Research Paper Series (University of Wisconsin Law School), Paper No. 1054 (October 2007), pp. 7-8, discussing, *inter alia*, political risk.

[40]See Berger et al. (2013), p. 268.

[41]See in particular Bonnitcha et al. (2017), pp. 164–166, with references to studies, concluding that "[t]he results are mixed. Taken together, the literature suggests that investment treaties do have some impact on *some* investment decisions in *some* circumstances, but that they are unlikely to have a large effect on the majority of foreign investment decisions".

[42]See, e.g. Frenkel and Walter (2019), pp. 1316–1342.

[43]See Berger et al. (2013), p. 268; See also Berger et al. (2011), pp. 270–272.

[44]See, e.g., Yackee (2008), pp. 808–809 and 827–828; Berger et al. (2011), p. 272.

some of these studies[45] as one of the bases for its recommendation that Australia no longer include investment arbitration in its future IIAs.[46]

By contrast, a different line of research identifies a positive impact of IIAs on FDI inflows, particularly when treaties include investment arbitration mechanisms.[47] Some scholars suggest that, among the various IIA provisions, investor-State arbitration clauses matter the most for foreign direct investment flows.[48] A 2016 research report conducted by the Asian Development Bank concluded that "BITs specifically granting access to [investor-State arbitration] have large, positive, and statistically significant effects on FDI".[49] A 2017 study covering a large number of countries and surveying different types of dispute settlement clauses similarly concludes that "stronger international dispute settlement provisions in BITs are indeed associated with more FDI activity".[50] **28.**

In conclusion, the empirical literature, based both on econometric and survey data, is not entirely conclusive on the extent to which IIAs in general and investor-State arbitration provisions in particular result in increased FDI. **29.**

2.2.2.2 De-Politicizing Disputes

"De-politicization" is often mentioned as one of the reasons for the establishment of the investment arbitration regime and celebrated as one of its central achievements.[51] **30.**

[45]Australian Government Productivity Commission (2010), *Bilateral and Regional Trade Agreements*, Research Report, pp. xxxvi, and 269–271 available at: https://www.pc.gov.au/inquiries/completed/trade-agreements/report/trade-agreements-report.pdf.

[46]See Shiro Armstrong and Luke Nottage (2016), *The Impact of Investment Treaties and ISDS Provisions on Foreign Direct Investment: A Baseline Econometric Analysis*, Sydney Law School Legal Studies Research Paper No. 16/74 (August 2016), p. 2.

[47]See Kerner (2009), p. 95.

[48]See, e.g., Angus Armstrong and Julian Winkler (2017), *Foreign Investment and Shared Sovereignty*, National Institute of Economic and Social Research Discussion Paper No. 475 (July 2017). See also Asian Development Bank (2016), *ASEAN Economic Integration Report 2016*, p. 163.

[49]Asian Development Bank, *ASEAN Economic Integration Report 2016*, p. 163 (with reference to Tables 6.28 and 6.29).

[50]Frenkel and Walter (2019), p. 1335. See also Shiro Armstrong and Luke Nottage (2016), *The Impact of Investment Treaties and ISDS Provisions on Foreign Direct Investment: A Baseline Econometric Analysis*, Sydney Law School Legal Studies Research Paper No. 16/74, August 2016, p. 24, finding "evidence that BITs do have a significant and positive impact on FDI flows from OECD countries to their partner host countries"; Rodolphe Desbordes (2017), *A Granular Approach to the Effects of Bilateral Investment Treaties and Regional Trade Investment Agreements on Foreign Direct Investment*, ABD Working Paper, arguing that BITs specifically granting access to an investor-State dispute mechanism and regional trade investment agreements specifically protecting foreign investors from discrimination have a large, positive, and statistically significant effect on FDI.

[51]As noted by Paparinskis, "[t]he contemporary State practice, case law and legal writings consider it almost axiomatic that depoliticisation is the purpose of investment protection regime" (see Paparinskis 2010, pp. 271–272). For instance, Michael Reisman argues that the "central

When discussing de-politicization in this context, investor-State arbitration is contrasted with diplomatic protection which, in the pre-investment treaty era, was a common means for investors to secure protection of their foreign investments and obtain reparation for the wrongful act inflicted by host States.[52] "De-politicization" more specifically is understood to refer to the removal of investment disputes from the realm of diplomatic protection in favor of a judicial forum subject to legal rules and a pre-formulated dispute settlement process.[53]

31. Although the views on de-politicization as a desirable feature of investor-State arbitration are not unanimously shared,[54] and opinions diverge as to whether the rise of investor-State arbitration has *actually* de-politicized disputes,[55] it can hardly be doubted that the shift from diplomatic protection to investment arbitration has entailed important consequences for investors, host States, and home States.

32. From the viewpoint of investors, access to an international judicial mechanism removes two major shortcomings associated with diplomatic protection. First, under the traditional conception, the right to exercise diplomatic protection belongs to the home State of the injured national,[56] and the State enjoys full discretion to pursue the claim or not.[57] The home State can decide not to exercise diplomatic protection for reasons unrelated to the merits of the claim, for instance, if making a claim would

---

achievement" of the investment treaty regime is the insulation of investor-State claims from "the caprice of sovereign-to-sovereign politics". See *Republic of Ecuador v. United States of America, Expert Opinion with Respect to Jurisdiction in the Interstate Arbitration Initiated by Ecuador Against the United States, W. Michael Reisman*, 24 April 2012, PCA Case No. 2012-5, para. 37. Similarly, Andreas Lowenfeld in his Separate Opinion in *CPI v. Mexico* posits that "[t]he essence of [investment treaties] is that controversies between foreign investors and host states are insulated from political and diplomatic relations between states". See *Corn Products International, Inc. v. United Mexican States*, ICSID Case No. ARB (AF)/04/1, Separate Opinion of Andreas F. Lowenfeld, 18 August 2009, para. 1. See also generally, Shihata (1986), pp. 1–32.

[52]In the words of the ILC, diplomatic protection consists in the "invocation by a State, through diplomatic action or other means of peaceful settlement, of the responsibility of another State for an injury caused by an internationally wrongful act of that State to a natural or legal person that is a national of the former State with a view to the implementation of such responsibility". See Article 1 of the International Law Commission (2006), *Draft Articles on Diplomatic Protection,* Official Records of the General Assembly, Sixty-first Session, Supplement No. 10, UN Doc. A/61/10.

[53]See, e.g., Kriebaum (2018), p. 15.

[54]For a conceptual critique of the de-politicization argument, see Paparinskis (2010), pp. 271–282.

[55]Compare Noel Maurer (2013), with Gertz et al. (2018), pp. 238–252 (who posit that the U.S. Government routinely intervenes in investment disputes where such intervention aligns with the U.S.' strategic interests). See also Joachim Pohl (2018), *Societal benefits and costs of International Investment Agreements: A critical review of aspects and available empirical evidence*, OECD Working Papers on International Investment, No. 2018/1, pp. 48–55.

[56]The Mavrommatis Palestine Concessions (1924) PCIJ Ser. A, No. 2, para. 21 where the Court held that "[b]y taking up the case of one of its subjects and by resorting to diplomatic action or international judicial proceedings on his behalf, a State is in reality asserting its own rights - its right to ensure, in the person of its subjects, respect for the rules of international law". See also Orrego Vicuña (2004), pp. 31–32.

[57]Barcelona Traction, Light and Power Company Limited (Belgium v. Spain), Judgment, I.C.J. Reports 1970, para. 79.

compromise its "diplomatic, military or geo-political objectives".[58] It also retains full control over the process (including the possibility to settle the claim) and any remedy awarded as a result of the exercise. Second, as a rule, "[a] State may not present an international claim in respect of an injury to a national or other person [...] before the injured person has [...] exhausted all local remedies".[59] The situation is markedly different in investor-State arbitration, where the aggrieved investor enjoys direct access to an international judicial forum, without depending on the intervention of its home State, has control of the process, directly benefits from any remedy awarded, and normally need not exhaust all local remedies.

The shift from diplomatic protection to investor-State arbitration is also said to benefit both the host State and the home State. Host States potentially avoid the risk of confrontations with the investor's home State.[60] For their part, home States may distance themselves from the investment dispute as the investor is able to litigate its claim directly without engaging the political organs of the two governments.[61] **33.**

While the objective of depoliticizing disputes is not easy to trace in the development of the IIA programs of many States,[62] "de-politicization was clearly on the minds of the architects of ICSID".[63] Aron Broches, the then General Counsel of the World Bank and principal architect of the Convention, repeatedly stressed that one of the primary goals of the Convention was "to remove investment disputes from the intergovernmental political sphere"[64] and presented the Convention as offering "a means of settling directly, on the legal plane, investment disputes between the State and foreign investor, [which] would insulate such disputes from the realm of politics and diplomacy".[65] The Convention further eliminated the requirement for the exhaustion of local remedies, unless otherwise agreed (Article 26) and significantly **34.**

---

[58]Newcombe and Paradell (2009), p. 6.

[59]Article 14, para. 1 of the International Law Commission (2006), *Draft Articles on Diplomatic Protection,* Official Records of the General Assembly, Sixty-first Session, Supplement No. 10, UN Doc A/61/10.

[60]See Schreuer et al. (2009), p. 416 (noting that "[d]iplomatic protection in investment disputes by capital exporting countries against developing countries has been a frequent source of irritation for the latter").

[61]Price (2011), p. 112; see also Price (2000), p. 427.

[62]In his extensive writings on the U.S. BIT program, former BIT negotiator Kenneth Vandevelde identifies de-politicization as one among several policy objectives of the architects of the U.S. investment treaty program (see, e.g. Vandevelde (2009), pp. 29–30; Vandevelde (1988), pp. 163–164). In respect of European States, it is argued that "[t]he objective of de-politicizing investment disputes played next to no role in the initiation and development of European BIT programmes". See Bonnitcha et al. (2017), p. 197.

[63]Bonnitcha et al. (2017), p. 198.

[64]See Broches (1995), p. 163, quoted in St John (2018), p. 103.

[65]ICSID (1968), pp. 242 and 303. Broches' successor Ibrahim Shihata also emphasized the depoliticization aspect of the Convention. See Shihata (1986), p. 5. On depoliticization during the negotiation of the Convention, see St John, who in her extensive review of the ICSID negotiating history argues that certain government officials participating in the negotiations "understood that claims about improving the investment climate or 'depoliticizing' investment disputes were to some

curtailed the possible exercise of diplomatic protection by the investor's home State (Article 27), thereby providing the host State with "the assurance that it will not be exposed to an international claim by the investor's home State, as long as it abides by the award".[66] These features were described during the negotiations of the ICSID Convention as "significant" and "important" innovations.[67]

2.2.2.3 An International Forum Alternative to Domestic Courts

35. A third reason that is normally said to justify the existence of an international remedy in favor of foreign investors is the need to offer an alternative to domestic courts.[68] Under usual choice of court rules, domestic courts would normally be the default forum for the settlement of investment disputes.[69] However, domestic courts are often considered inadequate for the settlement of investment disputes, due in particular to their perceived inefficiency, delays, actual or apparent bias to foreign investors, lack of independence from the host State, which is inevitably the respondent in the dispute, and lack of expertise to apply international law.[70]

36. Upon review of the *travaux* of the ICSID Convention, the purpose of establishing an international mechanism to provide an alternative to domestic courts appears to have played a relatively less important role compared to other goals (for instance the mentioned de-politicization of disputes). Nevertheless, the relationship between the envisaged dispute resolution machinery and domestic courts was raised on a number of occasions. Certain government delegates, especially from Latin American States, opposed the very idea of allowing a foreign investor direct access to an international forum.[71] At a meeting in Santiago, for instance, the Argentine and Brazilian delegates observed that the draft Convention would unacceptably confer to an international organization "powers belonging to national institutions" and grant foreign investors "a legally privileged position, in violation of the principle of full equality before the law".[72] In a similar vein, the expert-delegate from Jordan noted that "the

extent political window-dressing that helped make the idea of arbitration more palatable to capital importers" (St John 2018, p. 120).

[66] Schreuer et al. (2009), p. 416.

[67] ICSID (1968), pp. 164, 242, 403.

[68] See, e.g., Schreuer (2010), p. 71 ("One of the main purposes of investment arbitration is to avoid the use of domestic courts").

[69] Schreuer et al. (2009), p. 5.

[70] See, e.g., Schreuer (2010), pp. 71–72; Bjorklund (2007), pp. 253–256; Schill (2009), pp. 152–153; Schill (2010), p. 33.

[71] See Parra (2012), pp. 54–55. After the conclusion of the ICSID Convention, a number of States remained uncomfortable with the idea of granting direct procedural rights to foreign investors. No Latin American State, for instance, became a party to the ICSID Convention in the 1960s or 1970s. See Newcombe and Paradell (2009), p. 50. Most Latin American States ratified the ICSID Convention in the 1990s, after they had started liberalizing their foreign investment policies. *Ibid.*

[72] ICSID (1968), pp. 308, 306.

present Convention seemed to [. . .] place a foreign investor in a better position than the local investor".[73] Sporadically, the point was also made that domestic courts were not inadequate to resolve investment disputes.[74]

Broches responded to some of these doubts by explaining that "the proposed new machinery should not be a substitute for local courts and local law".[75] In his words: **37.**

> International proceedings became important in the abnormal case, where the normal ways of dealing with disputes proved unsatisfactory, perhaps because of a lack of governmental or judicial stability; perhaps because new legal relationships were being created for which there was as yet no appropriate or competent local forum. Implicit in the convention was the thought that it would be used only in these and other "appropriate cases".[76]

The same idea was then reflected in the Convention's preamble, which reads as follows: **38.**

> Bearing in mind the possibility that from time to time disputes may arise in connection with such investment between Contracting States and nationals of other Contracting States;
>
> Recognizing that while such disputes would usually be subject to national legal processes, international methods of settlement may be appropriate in certain cases [. . .].[77]

Thus, the Convention was not intended to displace dispute resolution before domestic courts; rather, it was conceived to provide an alternative dispute resolution mechanism to be used in appropriate circumstances, where the host State and the investor agreed to it.[78] However, once the parties consent to arbitration under the Convention, such consent shall exclude "any other remedy",[79] including domestic courts.[80] Furthermore, the exhaustion of local remedies is not a condition for resort to arbitration under the Convention unless it is specifically required by the host State.[81] **39.**

---

[73]See ICSID (1968), p. 549. See also St John (2018), p. 165.

[74]See, e.g., ICSID (1968), p. 473 (noting that the Australian delegate pointed out that "in practice the remedies provided in Australia by the local courts had to date proved satisfactory to foreign investors").

[75]ICSID (1968), p. 58.

[76]ICSID (1968), p. 58.

[77]ICSID Convention, preamble. See also Report of the Executive Directors on the Convention on the Settlement of Investment Disputes Between States and Nationals of Other States, Section III, 18 March 1965, paras. 10–11.

[78]See Schreuer et al. (2009), p. 6.

[79]See ICSID Convention, Article 26, first sentence (providing that "Consent of the parties to arbitration under this Convention shall, unless otherwise stated, be deemed consent to such arbitration to the exclusion of any other remedy").

[80]See Schreuer et al. (2009), pp. 351–352.

[81]See Article 26 of the ICSID Convention, second sentence (providing that "[a] Contracting State may require the exhaustion of local administrative or judicial remedies as a condition of its consent to arbitration under this Convention"). See also Schreuer et al. (2009), p. 352.

2.3 Outlook: Does Investment Law Still Need an International Dispute Resolution System?

40. With the UNCITRAL WGIII reform process underway, questions on the continued desirability of international mechanisms for the resolution of investment disputes are likely to resurface. These questions are expected to be raised in respect of *any* method in which individuals are allowed to bring international claims against States in their own name, be it investment arbitration, improved through targeted reforms or supplemented with an AM, or a MIC, all of which grant or would grant individuals standing before an international forum.

41. As States debate different reform proposals, they should in particular consider what function international tribunals are to serve and what alternatives foreign investors will have in the absence of an international mechanism. The answers to these questions may vary depending on the emphasis that each State places on its various roles as capital exporter, capital importer, protector of its nationals investing abroad, and potential respondent against claims brought by foreign investors.[82] The answer for each State may also depend on the particular treaty partner it faces in a specific IIA negotiation, as issues may be viewed differently depending on whether or not the negotiating States share common legal traditions and comparable cultural histories,[83] and/or place mutual trust in each other's institutions and in particular the judiciary.

42. The question of the function of international tribunals in the area of investment law is linked to whether IIAs and their dispute resolution provisions result in an increase in foreign investment. If one were to conclude that no such positive effect can be observed, it could be argued that the costs for States of keeping in place such a system exceed the benefits. In addition, absent a sound economic rationale, the "double procedural track" for foreign and domestic investors would be more difficult to justify as the modern eye generally disfavors discriminations and the two categories of investors may not always be seen to be in sufficiently different situations to warrant different treatment.

43. In light of the current uncertainty in the research on these matters and the perhaps insurmountable methodological and measurement challenges associated with it, some scholars underscore that it is unrealistic to expect that IIAs and/or dispute settlement provisions granting investors direct rights can alone result in increased FDI in the States that sign those treaties.[84] It is rather more likely that several factors influence an investor's decision to commit resources in a foreign country (including

---

[82]See Pearsall (2018), pp. 249–254.

[83]For instance, when agreeing to its FTA with Australia, which does not provide for investor-State dispute settlement, the United States justified this choice based on the "unique circumstances of this Agreement – including, for example, the longstanding economic ties between the United States and Australia, their shared legal traditions, and the confidence of their investors in operating in each other's markets [. . .]". See Dodge (2006), pp. 24–25.

[84]Dolzer and Schreuer (2008), p. 8.

the prospects for profits, tax regime, and general investment climate). However, to the extent that investors take into account the stability of the legal framework, the presence of IIAs and especially the availability of treaty-based mechanisms that stand outside the judicial system of the host State are likely to play a role in their decision to invest.

Seen from this perspective, the presence of an international mechanism for dispute resolution may serve as an important "confidence and credibility-inspiring signal"[85] to foreign investors and would enable host States to be credible when making commitments vis-à-vis foreign investors.[86] To the extent that foreign investors view international dispute settlement mechanisms as part of a stable legal framework, it cannot be excluded that the absence of such a mechanism may result in decisions not to invest. This was acknowledged, for instance, by the Australian government in its policy statement announcing its intention to do away with investor-State arbitration in the following terms: "If Australian businesses are concerned about sovereign risk in Australian trading partner countries, they will need to make their own assessments *about whether they want to commit to investing in those countries*".[87] In a similar vein, it is also possible that companies may restructure their investments in countries where international dispute settlement mechanism remain available in their treaties, which may entail the removal of those investors from the regulatory and taxation regimes of their "real" home States.[88] **44.**

When assessing the stability of the legal framework before investing in a country, investors may value the presence of IIAs and of an international dispute settlement method not only for the direct remedy it affords them against the host State, but also for the likely influence which the existence of such substantive and procedural guarantees may exercise on the State's decision-making processes when dealing with foreign investments. Although there is no comprehensive empirical data showing this correlation so far and there is debate amongst scholars as to whether investment treaty law can have a transformative impact on governmental conduct and domestic legal and bureaucratic culture,[89] it is likely that authorities at least in States with a robust governance do assess the risks of international litigation and responsibility when designing measures that may affect foreign investments. This does not necessarily mean that State initiatives in the area will be frozen in a **45.**

[85]See Damon Vis-Dunbar and Henrique Suzy Nikiema, *Do Bilateral Investment Treaties Lead to more Foreign Investment?* Investment Treaty News, 30 April 2009, available at https://www.iisd.org/itn/2009/04/30/do-bilateral-investment-treaties-lead-to-more-foreign-investment/.

[86]See Schill (2010), pp. 29–50.

[87]See Australian Government (Department of Foreign Affairs and Trade), *Gillard Government Trade Policy Statement: Trading our way to more jobs and prosperity* (April 2011), p. 14.

[88]Trackman (2012), p. 982.

[89]See Joachim Pohl (2018), *Societal benefits and costs of International Investment Agreements: A critical review of aspects and available empirical evidence*, OECD Working Papers on International Investment, No. 2018/1; Sattorova (2018), Schultz and Dupont (2015), pp. 1147–1168; Jansen Calamita (2015), pp. 103–128; Schill (2015), pp. 81–102; Guthrie (2013), pp. 1152–1200.

so-called regulatory chill, but rather that they would be shaped in such a manner as to conform to the State's international obligations. If this is so, it is likely that the availability of an international remedy may end up preventing the occurrence of situations giving rise to disputes.

46. In its recent Opinion 1/17 on the compatibility of the investor-State dispute settlement mechanisms included in the CETA with EU law, the CJEU also viewed access to international tribunals as a tool aimed at "giv[ing] complete confidence" to investors of one Contracting Party "that they will be treated, with respect to their investments in the territory of the other Party, on an equal footing with the enterprises and natural persons of that other Party, and that their investments in the territory of that other Party will be secure".[90] The Court was notably unconvinced by the argument that CETA would create inequality between foreign (in that case, Canadian) and domestic (in that case, EU) investors, reasoning that the two situations are not comparable because domestic investors do not make "international" investments.[91] Far from considering access to an international remedy as an unfair advantage for foreign investors, the Court appeared to view the grant of preferential procedural rights as a means of leveling the playing field between foreign and domestic investors.[92] Importantly, the Court also held that "the independence of the envisaged tribunals from the host State and the access to those tribunals for foreign investors are inextricably linked to the objective of free and fair trade" encapsulated in both the EU treaties and the CETA.[93]

47. In assessing whether it is appropriate to maintain in place or create new international tribunals for the adjudication of investment disputes, States are also likely to consider what the alternatives would be.

48. First, as skeptics of the existing system have noted,[94] even in the absence of treaty-based mechanisms it would of course be open to investors to seek to negotiate that their preferred dispute resolution clauses (for instance arbitration) be incorporated in their contracts. However, it is possible that only investors with strong bargaining power vis-à-vis the host State will succeed in obtaining their preferred

[90]Opinion 1/17 *EU Canada Comprehensive Economic and Trade Agreement* [2019] ECLI:EU:C:2019:341, para. 199.

[91]Opinion 1/17 *EU Canada Comprehensive Economic and Trade Agreement* [2019] ECLI:EU:C:2019:341, paras. 180–181.

[92]Opinion 1/17 *EU Canada Comprehensive Economic and Trade Agreement* [2019] ECLI:EU:C:2019:341, para. 199 ("it must be observed that the purpose of inserting in the CETA provisions concerning non-discriminatory treatment and protection of investments, and the creation of tribunals that stand outside the judicial systems of the Parties to ensure compliance with those provisions, is to give complete confidence to the enterprises and natural persons of a Party that they will be treated, with respect to their investments in the territory of the other Party, on an equal footing with the enterprises and natural persons of that other Party, and that their investments in the territory of that other Party will be secure", emphasis added).

[93]Opinion 1/17 *EU Canada Comprehensive Economic and Trade Agreement* [2019] ECLI:EU:C:2019:341, para. 200.

[94]See the statement by U.S. Trade Representative Robert Lighthizer at hearing before the U.S. Congress Ways and Means committee, 21 March 2018, *supra* Chap. 2, footnote 13.

options, whereas small and medium size investors will not. This would create inequalities between different categories of foreign investors.[95]

A second option would be to resort to the traditional inter-State mechanisms that were available in the pre-investment treaty era, based on diplomatic protection.[96] However, concerns have been expressed by a number of scholars over the re-politicization of disputes which would ensue as a result of a whole-sale shift to inter-State mechanisms.[97] It has been argued that "[a]s these cases are not actually located at the inter-state level, they should not be framed as disputes between states".[98] In addition, investors would face the known drawbacks linked to diplomatic protection which is "sporadic, arbitrary in its incidence and prone to politicisation, as there is no control over the process or any form of remedy for the individual whose claim is espoused".[99] Moreover, "[d]iplomatic relations can only tolerate a limited number of intergovernmental disputes" and many disputes concerning in particular "small and medium-sized enterprises (SMEs) and non-governmental organizations (NGOs), will never be selected for a politicized state-to-state dispute".[100] In other words, it is likely that only powerful economic actors, with leverage over their governments, would be able to obtain intervention from their home State,[101] which would create further instances of inequalities. **49.**

Put another way, the grant of an international forum to foreign investors (in the form of arbitration or standing adjudicatory bodies, such as a MIC) *by way of treaty* levels the playing field between foreign investors that qualify under that treaty, irrespective of their individual leverage vis-à-vis the host State (when seeking to **50.**

---

[95]For an analysis of the different categories of investors who have used investor-State arbitration, see Susan Franck (2019), pp. 76–82. See in particular pp. 76–77 at which Franck notes that "11.4% of cases involved claims brought solely by individuals" and "that corporate investors, potentially larger with more resources than individuals, dominated [investment treaty arbitration]. Yet cases involving individuals were a notable subcomponent". See also OECD, Government Perspectives on Investor-State Dispute Settlement: A Progress Report, 14 December 2012, p. 7, available at https://www.oecd.org/daf/inv/investment-policy/ISDSprogressreport.pdf, which reports that "[f]ar from supporting the view that smaller claimants are excluded from ISDS, the survey shows that 22% of the claimants in both ICSID and UNCITRAL cases are either individuals or very small corporations with limited foreign operations (only one or two foreign projects)".

[96]See the statement by U.S. Trade Representative Robert Lighthizer at hearing before the U.S. Congress Ways and Means committee, 21 March 2018, *supra* Chap. 2, footnote 13.

[97]Freya Baetens (2015), *Transatlantic Investment Treaty Protection – A Response to Poulsen, Bonnitcha and Yackee*, Paper No. 4 in the CEPS-CTR project "TTIP in the Balance" and CEPS Special Report No. 103 / March 2015, p. 9; Bronckers (2015), pp. 660 and 674.

[98]Freya Baetens (2015), *Transatlantic Investment Treaty Protection – A Response to Poulsen, Bonnitcha and Yackee*, Paper No. 4 in the CEPS-CTR project "TTIP in the Balance" and CEPS Special Report No. 103 / March 2015, p. 9.

[99]Freya Baetens (2015), *Transatlantic Investment Treaty Protection – A Response to Poulsen, Bonnitcha and Yackee*, Paper No. 4 in the CEPS-CTR project "TTIP in the Balance" and CEPS Special Report No. 103 / March 2015, p. 9.

[100]Bronckers (2015), p. 659.

[101]See also Trackman (2012), p. 982 (arguing that "many foreign investors lack access to their home states due to the limited scale of their foreign investments and their lack of sophistication").

negotiate an international dispute settlement option in a contract) or their home State (when seeking to obtain diplomatic espousal).

51. Third, serious concerns have also been expressed about the complete removal of access to international mechanisms for foreign investors such that foreign investors would only have access to domestic remedies.

52. In this respect, States should carefully weigh the costs and benefits of entrusting disputes regarding cross-border investments solely to domestic courts. A thorough comparison between international remedies and domestic remedies should be carried out based on a number of possible parameters, such as costs, duration, efficiency, and independence/neutrality.[102] Of particular concern to States assessing whether to forfeit entirely recourse to international remedies for investors in favor of domestic courts is likely to be judicial independence, risk of government interference, and neutrality. Annual studies produced by various institutions show that courts in a large number of States still face significant problems with respect to judicial independence or at least with the perceptions of independence.[103]

53. Furthermore, it has been highlighted that problems of delays and even due process are seen in both developed and developing countries, as is shown by the human rights breaches that are not infrequently found by the various regional human rights courts, for instance the European Court of Human Rights (ECtHR) under Article 6 of the European Convention on Human Rights (ECHR).

54. Finally, if investment disputes are entrusted solely to domestic courts, it should not be underestimated that in many cases disputes will only be capable of being settled by reference to domestic law, not international law, as in a number of countries IIAs cannot be invoked directly before the local courts.[104] This means

[102]There is no comprehensive empirical evidence comparing costs and duration of international dispute settlement mechanisms (in particular investment arbitration) with litigation in domestic courts. See Bonnitcha et al. (2017), pp. 88–89.

[103]See in particular Klaus Schwab (2018), *World Economic Forum. The Global Competitiveness Report*, available at http://www3.weforum.org/docs/GCR2018/05FullReport/TheGlobalCompetitivenessReport2018.pdf. See also, the "Justice Scoreboard" prepared annually by the European Commission to monitor the independence, quality and efficiency of justice systems in the EU Member States, which notes that "[t]he perceived independence of the judiciary is a growth-enhancing factor, as a perceived lack of independence can deter investments" (see European Commission (2019), *The 2019 EU Justice Scoreboard*, May 2019, COM(2019) 198/2, p. 44), and also refers to a study indicating "a positive correlation between perceived judicial independence and Foreign Direct Investment flows in Central and Eastern Europe", p. 4. It is interesting to observe that, even in a highly developed area such as the European Union, whose Member States generally rank high in global charts concerning judicial independence and good governance generally, (see Klaus Schwab (2018), World Economic Forum The Global Competitiveness Report referred to above), the Commission identifies certain shortcomings and lack of perceived independence in the justice systems of some of the Member States (see European Commission, *The 2019 EU Justice Scoreboard* (EU 2019), pp. 44–46) and notes at p. 55 that "[a]mong the reasons for the perceived lack of independence of courts and judges, the interference or pressure from government and politicians was the most stated reason, followed by the pressure from economic or other specific interests".

[104]See *infra* at 3.2.2.1.

that in the absence of an international dispute resolution mechanism before which the substantive standards contained in IIAs may be invoked, in those countries in which IIAs cannot be directly invoked these standards would become a dead letter.

Two final points should be made. First, despite the fact that investment arbitrations have often made the headlines in the media, it should not be overlooked that the vast majority of disputes between foreign investors and host States are resolved in national courts, rather than before international tribunals.[105] Thus, continuing to make international dispute settlement available is unlikely to change this fact. Second, acknowledging that there may be continuing reasons to maintain or establish international remedies for investors (whether in the form of arbitral tribunals, with or without an AM, or a standing MIC) in no way prevents States from recalibrating the interplay between domestic courts and international mechanisms as they deem appropriate based on their policy preferences and perceived needs. This is examined in the next sections, which review the interactions between domestic courts and the international mechanisms in the existing system (*infra* at Chap. 3), and explore the possible interplay in future dispute resolution frameworks (*infra* at Chap. 4). **55**.

References

Allee T, Peinhardt C (2011) Contingent credibility: the impact of investment treaty violations on foreign direct investment. Int Organ 65(3):401–432

Berger A, Busse M, Nunnenkamp P, Roy M (2011) More stringent BITs, less ambiguous effects on FDI? Not a BIT! Econ Lett 112:270–272

Berger A, Busse M, Nunnenkamp P, Roy M (2013) Do trade and investment agreements lead to more FDI? Accounting for key provisions inside the black box. Int Econ Econ Policy 10 (2):248–275

Bjorklund AK (2007) Private rights and public international law: why competition among international economic tribunals is not working. Hast Law J 59:241–308

Bonnitcha J, Skovgaard Poulsen LN, Waibel M (2017) The political economy of the investment treaty regime. Oxford University Press

Broches A (1995) Settlement of investment disputes, address to the world conference on world peace through law. In: Broches A (ed) Selected essays: World Bank, ICSID, and other subjects of public and private international law. Martinus Nijhoff, p 163

Bronckers M (2015) Is investor–state dispute settlement (ISDS) superior to litigation before domestic courts? An EU view on bilateral trade agreements. J Int Econ Law 18:655–677

Chaisse J, Bellak C (2011) Do bilateral investment treaties promote foreign direct investment? Preliminary reflections on a new methodology. Transnl Corp Rev 3(4):3–10

Chaisse J, Bellak C (2015) Navigating the expanding universe of international treaties on foreign investment creation and use of a critical index. J Int Econ Law 18:79–115

Dodge WS (2006) Investor-state dispute settlement between developed countries: reflections on the Australia-United States Free Trade Agreement. Vanderbilt J Transnl Law 39(1):1–37

Dolzer R, Schreuer C (2008) Principles of international investment law, 1st edn. Oxford University Press, p 8

[105] See Bonnitcha et al. (2017), pp. 82, 84–85.

Franck S (2019) Arbitration costs, myths and realities in investment treaty arbitration. Oxford University Press, pp 76–82

Frenkel M, Walter B (2019) Do bilateral investment treaties attract foreign direct investment? The role of international dispute settlement provisions. World Econ 42(5):1316–1342

Galbraith J (2019) Contemporary practice of the United States relating to international law, NAFTA is renegotiated and signed by the United States. Am J Int Law 113(1):150–159

Gertz G, Jandhyala S, Poulsen LNS (2018) Legalization, diplomacy, and development: do investment treaties de-politicize investment disputes? World Dev 107:238–252

Guthrie BK (2013) Beyond investment protection: an examination of the potential influence of investment treaties on domestic rule of law. N Y Univ J Int Law Polit 45:1152–1200

ICSID (1968) History of the ICSID Convention: documents concerning the origin and formulation of the Convention on the Settlement of Investment Disputes between States and Nationals of Other States, vol II-1. ICSID, p 242, 303

Jansen Calamita N (2015) The rule of law, investment treaties and economic growth: mapping normative and empirical questions. In: Jowell J, Christopher Thomas J, van Zyl Smit J (eds) Rule of law symposium 2014: the importance of rule of law in promoting development. Singapore Academy of Law and Bingham Centre for the Rule of Law, pp 103–128

Johnson L, Volkov O (2013) Investor-state contracts, host-state "commitments" and the myth of stability in international law. Am Rev Int Arbitr 24(3):361–415

Kerner A (2009) Why should I believe you? The costs and consequences of bilateral investment treaties. Int Stud Q 53(1):73–102

Kleinheisterkamp J (2012) Investment protection and EU law: the intra- and extra-EU dimension of the Energy Charter Treaty. J Int Econ Law 15(1):85–109

Kriebaum U (2018) Evaluating social benefits and costs of investment treaties: depoliticization of investment disputes. ICSID Rev Foreign Invest Law J 33(1):14–28

Miles K (2013) The origins of international investment law: empire, environment and the safeguarding of capital. Cambridge University Press, pp 86–87

Neumayer E, Spess L (2005) Do bilateral investment treaties increase foreign direct investment to developing countries? World Dev 33(10):1567–1585

Newcombe A, Paradell L (2009) Law and practice of investment treaties: standards of treatment. Wolters Kluwer, pp 44–46

Noel Maurer C (2013) The Empire trap. The rise and fall of U.S. intervention to protect American Property Overseas, 1893–2013. Princeton University Press

Orrego Vicuña F (2004) International dispute settlement in an evolving global society: constitutionalization, accessibility, privatization (Hersch Lauterpacht Memorial Lectures 2001 - Lauterpacht Research Centre for International Law University of Cambridge). Cambridge University Press, pp 31–32

Paparinskis M (2010) The limits of depoliticisation in contemporary investor-state arbitration. In: Crawford J, Nouwen S (eds) Select proceedings of the European Society of International Law, vol 3. Hart, pp 271–282

Parra AR (2012) The history of ICSID. Oxford University Press, pp 54–55

Parvanov PP, Kantor M (2012) Comparing U.S. law and recent U.S. investment agreements: much more similar than you might expect. In: Sauvant KP (ed) Yearbook on international investment law & policy 2010–2011. Oxford University Press, pp 741–836

Pauwelyn J (2014) At the edge of chaos? Foreign investment law as a complex adaptive system, how it emerged and how it can be reformed. ICSID Rev Foreign Invest Law J 29(2):372–418

Pearsall P (2018) The role of the state and the ISDS trinity. AJIL Unbound 112:249–254

Price DM (2000) Some observations on chapter eleven of NAFTA. Hast Int Comp Law Rev 23:421–429

Price DM (2011) Chapter 11 - Private Party vs. Government, investor-state dispute settlement: Frankenstein or safety valve? Canada-US Law J 26:107–114

Sattorova M (2018) The impact of investment treaty law on host states: enabling good governance? Hart

Schill SW (2009) The multilateralization of international investment law. Cambridge University Press, pp 152–153

Schill SW (2010) Private enforcement of international investment law: why we need investor standing in BIT dispute settlement. In: Waibel M, Kaushal A, (Liz) Chung K-H, Balchin C (eds) The Backlash against investment arbitration. Wolters Kluwer, pp 29–50
Schill SW (2015) International investment law and the rule of law. In: Jowell J, Christopher Thomas J, van Zyl Smit J (eds) Rule of law symposium 2014: the importance of rule of law in promoting development. Singapore Academy of Law and Bingham Centre for the Rule of Law, pp 81–102
Schreuer CH (2010) Interaction of international tribunals and domestic courts in investment law. In: Contemporary issues in international arbitration and mediation: The Fordham Papers, vol 4, pp 71–94
Schreuer CH, Malintoppi L, Reinisch A, Sinclair A (2009) The ICSID Convention—a commentary, 2nd edn. Cambridge University Press, p 4
Schultz T, Dupont C (2015) Investment arbitration: promoting the rule of law or over-empowering investors? A quantitative empirical study. Eur J Int Law 25(4):1147–1168
Shihata IFI (1986) Towards a greater de-politicisation of investment disputes: the roles of ICSID and MIGA. ICSID Rev Foreign Invest Law J 1(1):1–32
St John T (2018) The rise of investor-state arbitration: politics, law, and unintended consequences. Oxford University Press, pp 154–161
Swenson DL (2005) Why do developing countries sign bilateral investment treaties? UC Davis J Int Law Policy 12:131–155
Tobin J, Rose-Ackerman S (2006) Bilateral investment treaties: do they stimulate foreign direct investment? Yale University Law School E-Publications, pp 1–42
Tortian A (2012) The impact of bilateral investment treaties and financial development on foreign direct investment: evidence from Eurasia. Paper Submission for the Armenian Economic Association Conference, Haigazian University, Yerevan, Armenia (13–14 October 2012), pp 21–22
Trackman L (2012) Choosing domestic courts over investor–state arbitration: Australia's repudiation of the Status Quo. UNSW Law J 35(3):979–1012
UNCTAD (2014) IIA Issue Note – Working Draft, the impact of IIA on FDI: an overview of empirical studies 1998–2014. UNCTAD, p 5
Van Harten G (2010) Five justifications for investment treaties: a critical discussion. Trade Law Dev 2(1):19–58
Vandevelde K (1998) Investment liberalization and economic development: the role of bilateral investment treaties. Columbia J Transnl Law 36:501–527
Vandevelde KJ (1988) Reassessing the Hickenlooper Amendment. Va J Int Law 29(1):115–168
Vandevelde KJ (2009) U.S. International investment agreements. Oxford University Press, pp 29–30
Yackee JW (2008) Bilateral investment treaties, credible commitment, and the rule of (international) law: do BITs promote foreign direct investment? Law Soc Rev 42:805–832

Chapter 3
The Interplay Between Investor-State Arbitration and Domestic Courts in the Existing IIA Framework

3.1 Introduction

The interrelation between investment arbitration and domestic courts is complex and versatile, varying from harmonious co-existence to reinforcing complementation, reciprocal supervision and, occasionally, competition and tension. This chapter provides an overview of the different ways in which the inter-relationship between domestic courts and investor-State arbitration occurs in the current IIA framework. It first looks at the allocation of jurisdiction over investment disputes between courts and arbitral tribunals and reviews the ways in which the current IIA framework seeks to regulate the jurisdictional interaction between domestic and international tribunals (*infra* at Sect. 3.2). Section 3.3 then reviews the role of national courts in support and control of investment tribunals. Finally, Sect. 3.4 provides an overview of the reciprocal scrutiny of investor-State tribunals over the conduct of domestic courts. **56**

As already noted in the introductory remarks (*supra* in Chap. 1), the main points of intersection between domestic courts and international investment tribunals examined in this study touch on issues of jurisdiction, admissibility, merits, and procedure. The questions reviewed thus extend over almost all aspects of the law of investment protection, both substantive and procedural. Many of these questions are controversial and have often given rise to splits in the jurisprudence. Given the breadth of the issues, the study's approach is to focus primarily on State practice as reflected in the conclusion of IIAs and the policies underlying the choices reflected in the treaties. By contrast, the study does not systematically deal with the tools available to arbitral tribunals in seeking to coordinate multiple proceedings, e.g. *lis pendens*, *res judicata*, or abuse of process. **57**

G. Kaufmann-Kohler, M. Potestà, *Investor-State Dispute Settlement and National Courts*, European Yearbook of International Economic Law,
https://doi.org/10.1007/978-3-030-44164-7_3

3.2 Allocation of Jurisdiction Between Investor-State Tribunals and Domestic Courts

3.2.1 Jurisdictional Overlaps Between National and International Courts

58 Multiple judicial institutions, national and international, may be authorized to adjudicate—i.e. have jurisdiction over—what in substance is one and the same dispute, namely a disagreement about a State measure that has caused certain harm. These jurisdictional overlaps between domestic courts and international tribunals are not confined to investment law; they also occur in other areas of international law.[1] In the field of investment law, they have, however, given rise to particular difficulties and complexities.

59 A few examples may illustrate the extent of the jurisdictional interactions between national courts and international tribunals in investment law. A first point of jurisdictional contact and potential tension occurs in the adjudication of contract and treaty claims. A foreign investor may enter into an investment contract with the host State or a State-owned entity to regulate the terms of its cross-border investment in the host State. That contract may be governed by a certain substantive law (often the host State's law) and, of special relevance here, contain a dispute resolution clause providing for the jurisdiction of the host State's domestic courts or for commercial arbitration with a seat in the host State.

60 In *SGS v. Philippines*, for instance, the contract between the Swiss investor and the Philippines contained a choice in favor of the courts of the Philippines. When the Philippines failed to make certain payments under the contract, the investor filed an ICSID arbitration against the State, relying on the dispute resolution clause contained in the Swiss-Philippines BIT and alleging that the Philippines' conduct breached the BIT standards. Faced with the respondent's jurisdictional objection that the dispute was purely contractual and thus subject to the Philippines' courts in accordance with the contract, the ICSID tribunal determined that "justice would be best served if the Tribunal were to stay the [proceedings before it] pending determination of the amount payable [under the contract], either by agreement between the parties or by the Philippine courts in accordance with [the contract]".[2] The *SGS v. Pakistan* dispute presented a similar situation. Here, the contract provided for domestic arbitration in Pakistan. After Pakistan had commenced contractual arbitration in Islamabad, SGS filed an ICSID arbitration under the Swiss-Pakistan BIT. Pakistan argued that SGS's claim was essentially a claim for breach of contract, which should be submitted to the exclusive jurisdiction of the arbitrator in Pakistan. The ICSID tribunal found that the forum selection clause in the contract did not

---

[1]See generally Shany (2007).

[2]See *SGS Société Générale de Surveillance S.A. v. Republic of the Philippines*, ICSID Case No. ARB/02/6, 29 January 2004, para. 175.

affect its jurisdiction to adjudicate treaty breaches based on the BIT.[3] These examples show the concurrent jurisdiction of domestic courts or commercial arbitral tribunals under the contract, on the one side, and investment treaty tribunals under the treaty on the other, when both categories of adjudicatory bodies are seized of claims that arise out of substantively the same State conduct.

In a second type of overlapping situation, a foreign investor may seek to vindicate its rights for the same allegedly wrongful conduct by the State under both an IIA and domestic administrative or constitutional law. In the dispute between the Swedish State-owned company Vattenfall and the Federal Republic of Germany arising out of the State's decision to phase out nuclear energy after Fukushima, for instance, Vattenfall brought an ICSID arbitration against Germany under the ECT, which is still pending at the time of writing.[4] At the same time, Vattenfall's German subsidiary brought a constitutional complaint (*Verfassungsbeschwerde*) before the Federal Constitutional Court of Germany (*Bundesverfassungsgericht*) alleging that the closure of nuclear plants was tantamount to expropriation and that the lack of compensation for the nuclear phase-out required by the German Atomic Energy Act was inconsistent with German constitutional law. In 2016, the German Constitutional Court held that the German legislative measures were "for the most part compatible with the Basic Law" (the German constitution or *Grundgesetz*) and did not amount to an expropriation, while certain restrictions contained in the law were contrary to the constitutional right to property as they did not provide for compensation.[5] **61**

In Spain, the changes to the regulatory framework in the solar (photovoltaic) energy sector effected through a series of regulatory and legislative measures enacted between 2010 and 2013 triggered a wave of investor-State arbitrations brought by foreign investors against the Kingdom of Spain under the ECT and have resulted, in certain instances, in findings of liability against the Government.[6] At the same time, investors and other actors complained that the same measures were contrary to Spanish administrative and constitutional law and seized both the Spanish Supreme Court (*Tribunal Supremo*) and Constitutional Court (*Tribunal Constitucional*).[7] Both the investment treaty tribunals and the Spanish courts have thus passed judgment on claims for alleged violations of similar principles of legal certainty and legitimate expectations. These principles were anchored, however, in **62**

[3]See *SGS Société Générale de Surveillance S.A. v. Islamic Republic of Pakistan*, ICSID Case No. ARB/01/13, Decision of the Tribunal on Objections to Jurisdiction, 6 August 2003. The tribunal found, however, that it did not have jurisdiction over purely contractual claims which did not also amount to breaches of the relevant BIT.

[4]See *Vattenfall AB and others v. Federal Republic of Germany*, ICSID Case No. ARB/12/12 (pending).

[5]See German Federal Constitutional Court, Judgment of the First Senate of 6 December 2016, 1 BvR 2821/11 (German version available at http://www.bverfg.de/e/rs20161206_1bvr282111.html and English version available at http://www.bverfg.de/e/rs20161206_1bvr282111en.html).

[6]See, e.g., *Eiser Infrastructure Limited and Energía Solar Luxembourg S.à r.l. v. Kingdom of Spain*, ICSID Case No. ARB/13/36, Final Award, 7 May 2017.

[7]See generally García-Castrillón (2016).

different legal regimes, namely international law, specifically an IIA, for the investment claims and domestic law, specifically administrative and constitutional law, for the domestic claims.[8] In an analogous fashion, Italy's and the Czech Republic's repeal of incentives granted to renewable energy operators gave rise to both domestic and investment treaty arbitrations. It appears that in the Italian domestic proceedings, petitioners asserted violations not only of Italian administrative and constitutional law, but also of international law, including the ECT and the ECHR.[9]

63 These few examples show that a State measure or conduct may potentially violate several sources of laws, each with its own system of remedies, and thus potentially open up multiple avenues for redress to aggrieved investors. As a result, international arbitral tribunals routinely examine domestic measures adopted by national governments under investment law standards, while national courts may review those same measures from the perspective of domestic constitutional, administrative, tax or civil law (and, less frequently, also from the perspective of international law if the latter can be directly invoked by private parties before domestic courts).[10] Cases before the national and international courts are not always brought by the same party, but may be pursued by closely related parties (such as shareholders, subsidiaries, parent companies, etc.), either consecutively or simultaneously.

64 Despite the fact that the disputes brought before these different fora are distinct and formally independent, because the parties are often non-identical, the "cause of action" or legal basis for the claims is different (domestic law v. IIA), and the remedies sought may be distinct (annulment of a regulation, declaration of constitutionality, monetary compensation), the essence of the dispute is often the same in that it bears on the same set of facts or measures and involves the same economic harm. In practice, the multiplicity of remedies poses potential problems of duplication of proceedings, which implies a waste of resources, risks of conflicting factual and legal determinations, and risks of double or multiple recovery, where compensation is an available remedy in the different sets of proceedings.

65 It should also not be overlooked that when State measures negatively affect an investment, in addition to investment arbitration based on an IIA, private parties may be entitled to bring a claim before a human rights court (e.g., the ECtHR) alleging the violation of human rights, in particular—as far as relevant here—the right to

---

[8] In certain of the Spanish domestic cases, the ECT was also invoked. See García-Castrillón (2016), pp. 6–7 (discussing the judgment of the Spanish Constitutional Court no. 270/2015, in which the petitioners also invoked provisions of the ECT).

[9] See *Greentech Energy Systems A/S, et al v. Italian Republic*, SCC Case No. V 2015/095, Final Award, 23 December 2018, para. 197 (where Italy argued that "several Italian administrative court actions were brought by parties [...] regarding the measures at issue in this arbitration" and that "claimants in those actions asserted violations of the Italian Constitution, the ECHR, the ECT, and certain EU directives"). With regard to the Czech measures in the renewable energy sector which gave rise to both domestic and investment treaty arbitrations, see, e.g., *Jürgen Wirtgen, Stefan Wirtgen, Gisela Wirtgen and JSW Solar (zwei) GmbH & Co. KG v. Czech Republic*, PCA Case No. 2014-03, Final Award, 11 October 2017, sections II.G, V.D(1)(h) and (2)(h).

[10] See the Spanish and Italian cases mentioned *supra* at the preceding footnotes and the discussion *infra* at Sect. 3.2.2.1.

property under Protocol 1 of the ECHR. In *Yukos v. Russia*, for instance, the claimants in the ECT investment arbitrations and/or certain related parties brought domestic actions before the Russian courts as well as proceedings in the ECtHR.[11]

Against this background of multiple litigation opportunities, how does the IIA framework deal with the competing jurisdiction of national and international courts over the same dispute (understood in substantive terms) concerning an investment? As will be seen from the following sub-sections, IIAs seek to regulate the allocation of jurisdiction between domestic courts and investment treaty arbitration in two broad ways. The treaty may offer a choice between domestic courts and international arbitration ("alternative" approach) (*infra* at Sect. 3.2.2) or it may require that domestic remedies be pursued or even exhausted prior to commencing arbitration proceedings ("sequential" approach) (*infra* at Sect. 3.2.3). Within those broad categories, States have devised several constellations to cater for different policy concerns. Despite a growing awareness of the jurisdictional overlaps between national and international courts, the rules contained in IIAs do not always appear satisfactory. Indeed, they do not always provide for a clear "division of labor" between domestic courts and international tribunals; often they do not cater for the fact that the legal basis and the parties in the two settings may not be the same; and do not clarify whether one forum may (or even must) consider its counterpart's decision, ultimately leaving these matters to the best judgment of courts and tribunals. **66**

3.2.2 *Domestic Courts and International Arbitration as Alternative Fora*

IIAs often offer investors an alternative between domestic courts and international investment arbitration. Among other issues, this option raises the question of whether IIAs can be directly invoked by investors before domestic courts (*infra* at Sect. 3.2.2.1). Furthermore, where the investor has the choice of submitting its investment dispute before the domestic courts or in international arbitration, some **67**

[11] See *Yukos Universal Limited (Isle of Man) v. The Russian Federation*, UNCITRAL, PCA Case No. AA 227, Interim Award on Jurisdiction and Admissibility, 30 November 2009, paras. 587–600. The same measures may also be concurrently reviewed in domestic courts, investment treaty arbitration, and in the inter-State WTO setting. See, for instance, the tobacco restriction measures implemented in Australia, which gave rise to both domestic court proceedings (*JT International SA v. Commonwealth of Australia British American Tobacco Australasia Limited v. The Commonwealth* [2012] High Court of Australia 43), investment treaty arbitration (*Philip Morris Asia Limited v. The Commonwealth of Australia*, UNCITRAL, PCA Case No. 2012-12, Notice of Arbitration, 22 June 2011), and WTO disputes (Australia—Certain Measures Concerning Trademarks and Other Plain Packaging Requirements Applicable to Tobacco Products and Packaging, WT/DS434,WT/DS435,WT/DS441 (complaints initiated by the Dominican Republic, Honduras, and Ukraine on 18 July 2012, 4 April 2012, and 13 March 2012, respectively)). On jurisdictional overlaps between investment treaty and WTO disputes, see Allen and Soave (2014), pp. 1–58.

IIAs seek to minimize the risk of duplication of proceedings through fork-in-the-road or waiver clauses (*infra* at Sect. 3.2.2.2).

3.2.2.1 Domestic Courts as a Possible Forum for Disputes Under the IIA?

68 Regardless of whether an IIA mentions the host State's domestic courts as a forum for the adjudication of investment disputes between investors and States, those courts would normally be the default forum. Indeed, under usual choice of court rules, the proper forum would be that of the defendant, i.e. the host State, which also happens to be the place where the investment was made.[12] In fact, although there are no precise figures in this respect,[13] many disputes relating to an investment are resolved before domestic courts by reference to domestic law standards. Where the investor has the option of taking up an arbitration offer contained in an investment treaty, absent other direct arrangements with the State (e.g., an arbitration clause in a contract) the investor remains free to seize the domestic courts of its investment dispute, until it has taken up that offer. When it accepts the offer and consent to arbitration is perfected, limitations to bring the dispute before domestic courts may come into play depending on the applicable legal framework, for instance as a result of Article 26 of the ICSID Convention (which provides that "[c]onsent of the parties to arbitration under this Convention shall, unless otherwise stated, be deemed consent to such arbitration *to the exclusion of any other remedy*"), or of provisions contained in an IIA, such as a fork-in-the road or waiver clause (on which see *infra* at Sect. 3.2.2.2).

69 It is not uncommon for IIAs to mention expressly that domestic courts are a possible forum alternative to the international arbitration options provided under the treaty. The Switzerland-Tajikistan BIT (2009), for instance, provides that in respect of a "dispute with respect to investments between a Contracting Party and an investor of the other Contracting Party", "the investor may submit the dispute either to the national jurisdiction of the Contracting Party in whose territory the investment was made or to international arbitration".[14] Other IIAs provide that disputes "concerning an obligation under the treaty" (or similar formulations) can be brought before domestic courts or international arbitration. As an example, the Switzerland-Trinidad and Tobago BIT (2010) sets out that "the investor may submit the dispute [concerning an obligation under this Agreement] either to the courts or the administrative tribunals of the Contracting Party in whose territory the investment has been made or to international arbitration".[15]

---

[12] See Dolzer and Schreuer (2012), p. 235.

[13] See the discussion in Bonnitcha et al. (2017), p. 82.

[14] See Switzerland-Tajikistan BIT (2009), Article 11, paras. 1–2.

[15] Switzerland-Trinidad and Tobago BIT (2010), Article 8, para. 2.

In respect of these IIA formulations presenting domestic courts and investment treaty tribunals as adjudicative alternatives, the question arises whether an investor may invoke the substantive standards contained in the IIA before the local courts, rather than merely litigate its dispute by application of domestic law.[16] Whether there is scope for the application of IIAs by domestic courts depends on the text of the treaty and each domestic legal system. **70**

Treaties (or the domestic instruments accompanying their ratification)[17] rarely specify their own domestic law effects.[18] The answer to the question of whether the provisions of an IIA can be relied upon by private parties before domestic courts (or, **71**

[16]Examples of direct application of IIAs (or their "predecessors", the friendship, commerce, and navigation (FCN) treaties) before domestic courts of some countries have been documented, though they are not frequent. See Kjos (2016), pp. 81–96. See also Elettronica Sicula S.p.A. (ELSI) (Italy v. U.S.), Judgment, 1989 I.C.J. Rep. 15, 28 I.L.M. 1109 (July 20), paras. 61–62, where the chamber of the ICJ addresses Italy's position that individuals had been able to invoke provisions of FCN treaties before the Italian courts. See also *supra* Chap. 3, footnotes 8 and 9.

[17]See, e.g., U.S.-Rwanda BIT (2008), in which the U.S. Senate's report contains the following statements: "The resolution of advice and consent contains a statement reflecting the committee's understanding of the extent to which this Treaty will be self-executing. This provides that Articles 3-10 of the Treaty are self-executing and *do not confer private rights of action enforceable in United States courts*." (emphasis added). U.S. Congress, Investment Treaty With Rwanda, Senate Exec. Report 112-2, 12th Congress, 1st Session, 2 August 2011, 11 available at https://www.foreign.senate.gov/imo/media/doc/110-23.pdf. See also *ibid.*, 14 the "Text of Resolution of Advice and Consent to Ratification" at Title VII, Section 2, last sentence whereby "[n]one of the provisions in this Treaty confers a private right of action". A further example can be seen in the U.S.-Australia FTA (2004), which does not provide for investment arbitration, but merely State-to-State dispute settlement, and for which the U.S. implementing legislation provides that "[n]o person other than the United States [. . .] shall have any cause of action or defense under the Agreement [...] or may challenge [. . .] any action or inaction by any department, agency, or other instrumentality of the United States, any State, or any political subdivision of a State, on the ground that such action or inaction is inconsistent with the Agreement". See United States-Australia Free Trade Agreement Implementation Act, Public Law No 108-286, Sections 102(c)(1)-(2), 118 Statute 919 (2004) (codified at 19 USC section 3805 note). The U.S.-Australia FTA (2004) thereby entails that the substantive standards of protection can only be invoked in a State-to-State diplomatic protection scenario and not before the domestic courts, as noted by Dodge (2006), pp. 25–26.

In the context of the ECT, Article 26, paras. 1-2, provides that the investor has the choice to submit disputes "which concern an alleged breach of an obligation of the [host Contracting Party] under Part III" of the ECT "(a) to the courts or administrative tribunals of the Contracting Party party to the dispute". This provision of the ECT is accompanied by an "Understanding no. 16" whereby "Article 26(2)(a) should not be interpreted to require a Contracting Party to enact Part III of the Treaty into its domestic law". See generally on this De Luca (2016), available at http://rivista.eurojus.it/direct-effect-of-eus-investment-agreements-and-the-energy-charter-treaty-in-the-eu/ (arguing that "Understanding 16 seems to assume that Part III has direct effect within the domestic legal systems of the Contracting Parties, rather than the opposite").

[18]See Bronckers (2015), pp. 662–664. However see, for instance, CETA, providing that "[n]othing in this Agreement shall be construed as [. . .] permitting this Agreement to be directly invoked in the domestic legal systems of the Parties" (Article 30.6.1) and that "[a] Party shall not provide for a right of action under its domestic law against the other Party on the ground that a measure of the other Party is inconsistent with this Agreement" (Article 30.6.2). Consistent with this approach, the dispute settlement provisions in the investment chapter of the treaty provide that the investor may

in the parlance of certain jurisdictions, whether the treaty provides for a "private right of action" or "private cause of action" before the local courts) is thus left to the legal systems of each treaty party.[19]

72 In the United States, for instance, the U.S. Supreme Court has held that "[e]ven when treaties are self-executing in the sense that they create federal law, the background presumption is that '[i]nternational agreements, even those directly benefiting private persons, generally do not create private rights or provide for a private cause of action in domestic courts'".[20] Based on this holding, certain U.S. courts have concluded that a private party has no "standing to sue under the treaty" where the treaty in question had "no express language to rebut a presumption against a private right of action".[21]

73 Courts of other States, including Switzerland, have resorted to a number of criteria to determine whether provisions in a treaty can be directly invoked by individuals before the domestic courts. The Swiss Federal Tribunal, for instance, requires the provision at issue to be "sufficiently clear and precise so as to serve as the basis of a decision in a specific case", and "susceptible of application in court"; be concerned with "rights and obligations of private parties"; and "be addressed to the authorities charged with the application of the law" rather than the legislator.[22]

74 If an IIA were to be invoked before the Swiss courts, it would seem that the very fact that the treaty affords the investor an option to file its treaty claims in the domestic courts of the host State in and of itself implies that the treaty standards are susceptible of being applied by a court, regardless of the criteria just referred to. A contrary conclusion would be difficult to reconcile with the State's undertaking in

---

only bring a claim for alleged breaches of the CETA investment protection standards before the international tribunal constituted under the treaty, and not before domestic courts.

[19]The question as to whether an individual may invoke a treaty before domestic courts should be distinguished from the so-called "self-executing" nature of treaties (i.e., treaties that create a legal obligation in the absence of implementing legislation). See Hathaway et al. (2012), p. 56, also referring to Restatement (Third) of Foreign Relations, section 111 cmt. G (1987) (whereby "[w]hether a treaty is self-executing is a question distinct from whether the treaty creates private rights or remedies"). See also Kaiser (2013), paras. 1–3.

[20]*Medellin v. Texas*, 522 US 491 (2008).

[21]See Hathaway et al. (2012), pp. 70–76 (discussing U.S. cases applying treaties, including FCN treaties, after the Supreme Court case in *Medellin*, quoted above in the text).

[22]See, e.g., Swiss Federal Tribunal, *L.X. v. M.F*, decision of 22 December 1997, 90, 91, para. 3 (a) (a provision in a treaty must be regarded as directly applicable "wenn die Bestimmung inhaltlich hinreichend bestimmt und klar ist, um im Einzelfall Grundlage eines Entscheides zu bilden; die Norm muss mithin justiziabel sein, die Rechte und Pflichten des Einzelnen zum Inhalt haben, und Adressat der Norm müssen die rechtsanwendenden Behörden sein"/"Pour qu'une règle soit directement applicable, il faut que le contenu de la disposition en cause soit suffisamment clair et précis pour servir de fondement à une décision d'espèce. La règle doit donc être susceptible d'application sur le plan judiciaire, porter sur des droits et des devoirs particuliers et s'adresser aux autorités chargées de l'application du droit"). See also Swiss Federal Tribunal, *D. v. Familienausgleichskasse Zug*, decision of 31 August 2010, 297, 307–308, para. 8.1; Swiss Federal Tribunal, *Schmid und Mitb. v. Regierungsrat und Grossen Rat des Kantons Basel-Stadt*, decision of 7 August 2007, 286, 291, para. 3.2. See generally, Besson (2016), pp. 333–337.

the treaty "that the investor may submit the dispute concerning an obligation under the IIA either to the courts of the Contracting Party in whose territory the investment has been made or to international arbitration". It would also be astonishing that domestic courts could not apply treaty standards, for instance because they would be regarded as insufficiently clear or precise, when the same standards are expected to be applied—and are routinely applied—by arbitral tribunals. Because of the very nature of IIAs, which confer rights on private parties and impose obligations on States vis-à-vis these private parties, the same solution should prevail, i.e. domestic courts should be in a position to apply the IIA, even when the treaty does not expressly provide for the possibility to submit claims arising out of the treaty to national courts.

3.2.2.2 Fork-in-the-Road and Waiver Clauses

IIAs may seek to coordinate domestic and international proceedings in respect of the same investment dispute through so-called "fork-in-the-road" clauses and "waiver"/ "no U-turn" provisions.[23] **75**

Through a fork-in-the-road clause, States wish to make sure that, where the investor has a choice between domestic courts and international arbitration, the investor's choice once made is final. In other words, if the fork-in-the-road is triggered, the investor may only continue to pursue its claim in the forum to which it has first turned (*electa una via, non datur recursus ad alteram*).[24] In still other words, once the choice is made, the alternative forum becomes exclusive. **76**

Fork-in-the-road clauses may entail different consequences depending on their wording. Some may make the choice of either domestic courts or international arbitration irreversible, whatever forum is seized first. The Switzerland-Colombia BIT, for instance, provides that "[o]nce the investor has referred the dispute to either a national tribunal or any of the international arbitration mechanisms provided for in paragraph 2 above, the choice of the procedure shall be final".[25] Other treaties prescribe that only the choice of domestic courts is final.[26] Alternatively, the investor's choice between international arbitration and domestic court proceedings **77**

[23]Some BITs, however, provide that the investor can access domestic courts and investment arbitration one after the other. See Germany-Madagascar BIT (2006), Article 11, para. 2.

[24]Schreuer (2004), pp. 239–240.

[25]Switzerland-Colombia BIT (2006), Article 11, para. 4. See also Switzerland-Egypt BIT (2010), Article 12, para. 6, ("Once the investor has submitted the investment dispute to one of the fora referred to in paragraph (3), that election is final").

[26]See, e.g., Switzerland-Saudi Arabia BIT (2006), Article 10, para. 3 (providing that "[i]f the dispute has been filed with the competent court of the Contracting Party in accordance with paragraph (2) of this Article, the investor may not submit this dispute to international arbitration as referred to in the same paragraph").

may be reversible until the first instance domestic court has issued its judgment, but not later.[27]

78 The ECT provides for a choice of several fora, including domestic courts and international arbitration. The treaty offers the Contracting Parties the possibility to opt into the fork-in-the-road clause pursuant to Article 26, para. 3(b)(i), and, specifically, to limit their consent to international arbitration only to disputes which the investor has not previously submitted to the domestic courts (or other previously agreed dispute settlement procedure). A number of Contracting Parties, including the European Union, some of its Member States, and Japan, have availed themselves of this possibility and provided written statements under Article 26, para. 3(b)(ii) of their "policies, practices and conditions" in respect of the application of the fork-in-the-road clause.[28] With regard to States such as Switzerland who have made no such statement under Article 26, para. 3(b)(ii), the investor's prior initiation of domestic court proceedings does not prevent the investor from subsequently launching an international arbitration against that State.[29]

79 A different type of approach to the coordination of multiple proceedings before domestic and international fora is to include "waiver" or "no-U-turn" clauses. Unlike fork-in-the-road clauses (which make the choice of forum by the investor final), waiver or no-U-turn provisions permit investors to opt for international arbitration after commencing domestic court proceedings in relation to the same measure. However, if the investor decides to submit a claim to international arbitration

---

[27] See, e.g., Austria-Slovenia BIT (2001), Article 11, para. 4 (providing that "[t]he investor may choose to submit the dispute for resolution according to paragraph 2b [international arbitration] only until there has been a decision concerning the same claim in the first instance in the proceedings according to paragraph 2a [domestic courts]"); Austria-Mexico BIT (1998), Article 10, para. 2 (providing that "[i]f an investor of a Contracting Party or his investment that is an enterprise initiates proceedings before a national tribunal with respect to a measure that is alleged to be a breach of this Agreement, the dispute may only be submitted to arbitration under this Part if the competent national tribunal has not rendered judgment in the first instance on the merits of the case"). Similarly, the Switzerland-Turkey BIT (1988) appears to entitle the investor to initiate ICSID arbitration as long as the domestic court has not issued a final decision. See Switzerland-Turkey BIT (1988), Article 8, para. 3 (providing that "the dispute shall be submitted to [ICSID arbitration] [. . .], provided that in case the investor concerned has brought the dispute before the courts of justice of the Contracting Party that is a party to the dispute and there has not been rendered a final award [*sic*]").

[28] See Energy Charter Secretariat, "Transparency Document: Policies, Practices And Conditions Of Contracting Parties Listed In Annex ID Not Allowing an Investor to Resubmit the Same Dispute to International Arbitration at a Later Stage As Provided By Contracting Parties (in accordance with Article 26(3)(b)(ii) of the Energy Charter Treaty)", 10 June 2009, available at https://www.energychartertreaty.org/fileadmin/DocumentsMedia/Founding_Docs/June_2009_Annex_ID.pdf.

[29] See, e.g., *Petrobart Ltd v. Kyrgyz Republic*, SCC Case No 126/ 2003, Arbitral Award, 29 March 2005, p. 56 (noting that "even if Petrobart had submitted its claims based on the Treaty to any of the above fora (i.e. domestic court or UNCITRAL arbitration), which it did not, subsequent submission to arbitration under Article 26 would still have been permissible. This would have been the case because [. . .] the Kyrgyz Republic chose not to be listed in Annex ID of the Treaty").

under the dispute settlement provision in the IIA, it is required to discontinue domestic court proceedings or waive its right to start new such proceedings.

This type of provisions is typically contained in IIAs entered into by the U.S.[30] **80**
The Switzerland-China BIT also provides that "[a] dispute that has been submitted, in accordance with paragraph (2), to a competent court of the Contracting Party concerned, may only be submitted to international arbitration after withdrawal by the investor of the case from the domestic court".[31]

In broad terms, fork-in-the-road and waiver clauses pursue the same objectives: **81**
avoiding parallel proceedings, which entail duplication of costs, risks of double recovery and of inconsistent outcomes. Despite their common goals, the two types of clauses imply somewhat different policies and entail advantages and disadvantages. Fork-in-the-road clauses are aimed at avoiding that a dispute is litigated first before domestic courts, and then before an international tribunal (or vice versa). Their effect is to prevent, in principle, any duplication of proceedings and thus of costs, because the trigger of one forum automatically entails the loss of access to the other. They may, however, prompt investors to immediately access the international forum, for fear of otherwise losing that option if domestic proceedings are started. Waiver clauses, on the other hand, do not pre-empt nor discourage investors from seeking redress before national courts first, as they leave the investors' right to access the international forum intact, if for instance the domestic proceedings are deemed unsatisfactory. This may entail a waste of resources if domestic courts are accessed first and then those proceedings are discontinued once arbitration proceedings are commenced. However, because domestic court proceedings may lead to a satisfactory outcome of the dispute, waiver clauses may have the effect of reducing potential investment arbitration claims.

The interpretation of fork-in-the-road and waiver clauses has occupied arbitral **82**
tribunals who have been faced with numerous questions concerning their scope of application. In particular, questions as to whether identity is required between parties, object, and cause of action (so-called "triple identity test" transposed from *res judicata* and *lis pendens* requirements) in the domestic and international

[30]U.S.-CAFTA-DR (2004), Article 10.18, para. 2(b), for instance, requires the investor's notice of arbitration to be accompanied by a "written waiver" "of any right to initiate or continue before any administrative tribunal or court under the law of any Party, or other dispute settlement procedures, any proceeding with respect to any measure alleged to constitute a breach referred to in Article 10.16".

[31]Switzerland-China BIT (2009), Article 11, para. 4. See also Switzerland-Japan FTA (2009), Chapter 9, Article 94, para. 6(b). Sometimes, fork-in-the-road or waiver clauses specify that, regardless of the choice that the investor makes between one or the other forum, the investor is not prevented from applying to the host State's courts for provisional measures. See, e.g., Switzerland-Japan FTA (2009), Chapter 9, Article 94, para. 6, second sentence ("It is understood that a disputing investor may initiate or continue an action that seeks interim injunctive relief and does not involve the payment of monetary damages before a judicial or administrative tribunal of the disputing Party, provided that the action is brought for the sole purpose of preserving the disputing investor's rights and interests while the conciliation or arbitration is pending").

proceedings, have been invariably raised in investment jurisprudence.[32] The supposed requirement for an identity of cause of action has proven particularly problematic where the claims under the treaty were linked to contractual claims that had been made before domestic courts.[33]

83 A careful drafting of the clauses may clarify to the benefit of investors and States a number of uncertainties that have emerged in arbitral practice.[34] In particular, States may wish to consider the need to phrase fork-in-the-road and waiver clauses in broader terms than are currently provided in many IIAs, so as to cover concurrent or subsequent litigation by closely related parties (thus: not limited to the "same" party) in relation to the same facts or measures (thus: without regard to the legal basis invoked, which is often necessarily different in the two fora), aimed at achieving comparable remedies. In other words, the IIA language should aim at avoiding the limitations resulting from the application of the (too) narrow "triple identity" test, to the extent those limitations are considered inapposite. Furthermore, if States consider it appropriate, rules on coordination may extend beyond regulating domestic court and investment arbitration proceedings and cover overlaps with other *international* dispute settlement mechanisms providing for direct remedies to private parties (e.g., human right courts).[35] Many of the waiver clauses contained in U.S. treaties

---

[32]This is not the place to do justice to the copious jurisprudence. See generally Schreuer (2004), pp. 239–249; Wegen and Markert (2010), pp. 269–292.

[33]See, in particular, *Compañiá de Aguas del Aconquija S.A. and Vivendi Universal S.A. v. Argentine Republic*, 5 ICSID Reports 299, Award, 21 November 2000, paras. 55 and 81; *Compañiá de Aguas del Aconquija S.A. and Vivendi Universal S.A. v. Argentine Republic*, 6 ICSID Reports 340, Decision on Annulment, 3 July 2002, paras. 36-42, 55 and 113; *Alex Genin, Eastern Credit Limited, Inc. and A.S. Baltoil v. The Republic of Estonia*, ICSID Case No. ARB/99/2, Award, 25 June 2001, paras. 331–332; *Supervision y Control S.A. v. Republic of Costa Rica*, ICSID Case No. ARB/12/4, Final Award, 18 January 2017, paras. 308-321 and 330; *Yuri Bogdanov and Yulia Bogdanova v. Republic of Moldova*, SCC Case No V091/2012, Final Award, 16 April 2013, paras. 173–174; *Middle East Cement Shipping and Handling Co SA v. Arab Republic of Egypt*, ICSID Case No ARB/99/6, Award, 12 April 2002, para. 71; *Total SA v. Argentine Republic*, ICSID Case No ARB/04/01, Decision on Liability, 27 December 2010, para. 443; *Toto Costruzioni Generali SpA v. Republic of Lebanon*, ICSID Case No. ARB/07/12, Decision on Jurisdiction, 11 September 2009, paras. 211–212; *Occidental Exploration and Production Company v. Republic of Ecuador*, LCIA Case No UN3467, Final Award, 1 July 2004, paras. 57–58; *Pantechniki SA Contractors and Engineers v. Albania*, Award, ICSID Case No ARB/07/21, IIC 383 28 July 2009, paras. 61–64; *H&H Enterprises Investments, Inc. v. Egypt*, ICSID Case No. ARB/09/15, Award, 6 May 2014, paras. 356–382; See also *Woodruff Case*, IX RIAA 213, Venez. Mixed Claims Commission, 17 February 1903, pp. 222–223 (where the "fundamental basis" test was first articulated). See also Wegen and Markert (2010), p. 276.

[34]See for instance the recent EU-Viet Nam Investment Protection Agreement (2019) (not yet in force), Article 3.34; EU-Singapore Investment Protection Agreement (2018) (not yet in force), Article 3.7, paras. 1(f) and 2.

[35]By contrast, as explained by Allen and Soave, it is not possible to provide for fork-in-the-road clauses that govern WTO and investment claims arising out of the same measure, because "there is no 'fork-in-the-road' for either the home State or its investor to take. An investor cannot choose a WTO claim over an investment claim, or vice versa. The investor has no control over whether a State or group of States pursues a WTO claim with respect to the same measure. Nor does the home

already contain language that obliges the relevant party to waive or discontinue proceedings "with respect to the measure" not only "before any administrative tribunal or court under the law of any Party" but also before "*other dispute settlement procedures*".[36]

3.2.3 *Prior Recourse to Domestic Courts Before Resorting to Investment Arbitration*

A number of treaties coordinate domestic and international remedies through a "sequential" approach, by requiring investors to seize domestic courts before accessing the international forum. IIAs may incorporate the traditional exhaustion of local remedies requirement (*infra* at Sect. 3.2.3.1) or contain prior domestic litigation requirements short of exhaustion (*infra* at Sect. 3.2.3.2). **84**

3.2.3.1 Exhaustion of Domestic Remedies

Within the field of diplomatic protection, a State "may not bring an international claim in respect of an injury to a national [. . .] before the injured person has [. . .] exhausted all local remedies".[37] Various justifications have been given for the rule.[38] In the *Interhandel* case, the ICJ observed that the rule serves to ensure that "the State where the violation occurred should have an opportunity to redress it by its own means, within the framework of its own domestic system".[39] **85**

The rule requires the investor to exhaust any reasonably available remedy before administrative or judicial courts so long as the remedy is not "obviously futile".[40] This normally means obtaining the final judgment of the highest court of the host **86**

State have control over the investor's decision to assert an investment claim". See Allen and Soave (2014), p. 54.

[36]See, e.g., NAFTA, Article 1121, subsections (1)(b) and (2)(b); U.S.-CAFTA-DR (2004), Article 10.18, para. (2)(b).

[37]International Law Commission (2006), *Draft Articles on Diplomatic Protection,* Official Records of the General Assembly, Sixty-first Session, Supplement No. 10, UN Doc. A/61/10, Article 14(1).

[38]See Crawford and Grant (2007), para. 7.

[39]*Interhandel* (Switz. v. U.S.), Preliminary Objections, 1959 I.C.J. Rep. 6, (Mar. 21) p. 27.

[40]Finnish Shipowners (Finland) v. Great Britain (Use of Certain Finish Vessels during the War) (9 May 1934), III UNRIAA, 1479, pp. 1503–1505; International Law Commission (2006), *Draft Articles on Diplomatic Protection,* Official Records of the General Assembly, Sixty-first Session, Supplement No. 10, UN Doc. A/61/10, Article 15; *Certain Norwegian Loans* (France v. Norway), Judgment, 1957 I.C.J. Rep 9, (July 6), (separate opinion of Judge Lauterpacht), pp. 39–41.

State.[41] In order to satisfy the exhaustion of local remedies requirement, the domestic and international proceedings should be "designed to obtain the same result".[42] The form and the arguments of the claims before the domestic and international tribunal may be different, as long as "the essence of the claim has been brought before the competent tribunals and pursued as far as permitted by local law and procedures, and without success".[43]

87 In addition to the field of diplomatic protection, including inter-State claims under FCN treaties,[44] the rule continues to be applied to individual complaints of international human rights violations.[45]

88 The rise of IIAs has changed considerably the role of the exhaustion of local remedies rule in investment protection claims. Because IIAs and their dispute settlement rules provide for a direct right of the investor to bring claims against the host State, they are considered to "abandon or relax the conditions relating to the exercise of diplomatic protection, particularly the rules relating to [...] the exhaustion of local remedies".[46] As noted in the ILC Draft Articles on Diplomatic Protection, the rules on diplomatic protection do not apply "to the extent they are inconsistent with special rules of international law, such as treaty provisions for the protection of investments".[47]

89 Within the framework of the ICSID Convention, Article 26 of the Convention provides that:

> Consent of the parties to arbitration under this Convention shall, unless otherwise stated, be deemed consent to such arbitration to the exclusion of any other remedy. A Contracting State

[41]International Law Commission (2006), *Draft Articles on Diplomatic Protection with commentaries*, Report of the Fifty-Eighth Session, UN Doc. A/61/10, 2006/II(2) ILC Yearbook, Commentary to Article 14, para. 4.

[42]*Interhandel* (Switz. v. U.S.), Preliminary Objections, 1959 I.C.J. Rep. 6, (Mar. 21), p. 27.

[43]*Elettronica Sicula S.p.A. (ELSI)* (Italy v. U.S.), Judgment, 1989 I.C.J. Rep. 15, (July 20), para. 59.

[44]In the ELSI case before the ICJ, brought under the United States-Italy FCN treaty, the United States argued that the exhaustion of local remedies rule did not apply as it was not mentioned in the dispute settlement provision of the FCN Treaty. The ICJ found itself "unable to accept that an important principle of customary international law should be held to have been tacitly dispensed with, in the absence of any words making clear an intention to do so". See *Elettronica Sicula S.p.A. (ELSI)* (Italy v. U.S.), Judgment, 1989 I.C.J. Rep. 15, (July 20), para. 50.

[45]See International Covenant on Civil and Political Rights, (19 December 1966), 999 U.N.T.S. 171, Article 41, para. 1(c); Optional Protocol to the International Covenant on Civil and Political Rights, (19 December 1966), 999 U.N.T.S. 302, Article 5, para. 2(b); Convention for the Protection of Human Rights and Fundamental Freedoms (4 November 1950), 213 U.N.T.S. 221, Article 35, para. 1; American Convention on Human Rights, (22 November 1969), O.A.S.T.S. No. 36, Article 46, para. 1(a)–(b), 2; African (Banjul) Charter on Human and Peoples' Rights, (27 June 1981), O.A.U. Doc. No. CAB/LEG/67/3 rev. 5, 21 I.L.M. 58 (1982), Article 50.

[46]International Law Commission (2006), *Draft Articles on Diplomatic Protection with commentaries*, Report of the Fifty-Eighth Session, UN Doc. A/61/10, 2006/II(2) ILC Yearbook, Commentary to Article 17, para. 1.

[47]International Law Commission (2006), *Draft Articles on Diplomatic Protection,* Official Records of the General Assembly, Sixty-first Session, Supplement No. 10, UN Doc. A/61/10, Article 17.

may require the exhaustion of local administrative or judicial remedies as a condition of its consent to arbitration under this Convention.[48]

Article 26 reverses the situation under customary international law: under the Convention, Contracting States waive the requirement of exhaustion of local remedies unless otherwise stated.[49] The second sentence of Article 26 clarifies that a State may make the exhaustion of local remedies a condition of its consent to arbitration.[50] **90**

A few States have sought to re-instate the exhaustion requirement when acceding to or ratifying the Convention. According to the ICSID website,[51] Israel,[52] Costa Rica,[53] and Guatemala[54] have made such declarations.[55] **91**

State practice in concluding IIAs shows a diversity of approaches in respect of the exhaustion of local remedies rule. Broadly speaking, IIAs may (1) require exhaustion of local remedies; (2) waive exhaustion of local remedies; or (3) be silent on whether local remedies need to be exhausted prior to commencing arbitration proceedings. **92**

Starting with the first type of treaties,[56] the requirement to exhaust domestic remedies before resort to international arbitration can in particular be found in early treaties of the 1970s and 1980s.[57] By contrast, this feature has not appeared in BITs **93**

---

[48] Article 26 (emphasis added).

[49] Schreuer et al. (2009), p. 403.

[50] Schreuer et al. (2009), p. 403.

[51] See ICSID (2019), *Contracting States and Measures Taken By Them For The Purpose Of The Convention*, Doc. ICSID/8, February 2019, available at https://icsid.worldbank.org/en/Documents/icsiddocs/ICSID%208-Contracting%20States%20and%20Measures%20Taken%20by%20Them%20for%20the%20Purpose%20of%20the%20Convention.pdf.

[52] On 22 June 1983, Israel notified the Centre that, with reference to Article 26 of the Convention, "Israel requires the exhaustion of local administrative or judicial remedies as a condition under this Convention". This notification was withdrawn by Israel by a communication received by the Centre on 21 March 1991. See ICSID, "Contracting States And Measures Taken By Them For The Purpose Of The Convention", *supra* note 51, p. 1, footnote 5.

[53] On 27 April 1993, Costa Rica notified the Centre that "[t]here may only be recourse to arbitration pursuant to [the Convention] where all existing administrative or judicial remedies have been exhausted". See ICSID, "Contracting States And Measures Taken By Them For The Purpose Of The Convention", *supra* note 51, p. 1, footnote 5.

[54] On 16 January 2003, Guatemala notified the Centre that "the Republic of Guatemala will require the exhaustion of local administrative remedies as a condition of its consent to arbitration under the Convention". See ICSID, "Contracting States And Measures Taken By Them For The Purpose Of The Convention", *supra* note 51, p. 2, footnote 6.

[55] It has been argued that "a general notification of this kind is a statement for information purposes only. [...] If a State subsequently consents to ICSID arbitration in terms inconsistent with the prior general notification, the consent will prevail over the notification". See Schreuer et al. (2009), para. 194.

[56] On which see generally Schreuer (2010), pp. 73–74; Schreuer (2005), pp. 1–17; Brauch (2017), pp. 7–12.

[57] See, e.g., Malaysia-Netherlands BIT (1971), Article 12; Netherlands–Singapore BIT (1972), Article XI; Republic of Korea-Netherlands BIT (1974), Article 6; Germany–Israel BIT (1976),

concluded from 2004 to 2012.[58] One Swiss BIT conditioning consent to arbitration to exhaustion of local remedies "in accordance with international law" is the treaty with Jamaica of 1990.[59]

94 More recently, the exhaustion rule has re-appeared in treaties of a few States.[60] Notably, the new Indian Model BIT and a few of the recent treaties entered into by India modelled thereafter,[61] require "exhaustion" of "all judicial and administrative remedies" for 5 years.[62] Despite being termed as "exhaustion", the Indian rule is more akin to a prior litigation requirement (on which see *infra* at Sect. 3.2.3.2) as it does not require the investor to "exhaust" local remedies until the final instance, but calls for litigation of the dispute before the courts for a 5-year period of time.

95 For those treaties that expressly require exhaustion as a condition to the commencement of arbitration proceedings, the exceptions to the rule under customary international law are likely to apply, i.e. domestic remedies need not be exhausted where they would be "futile" or provide no "reasonable possibility of effective redress".[63] The treaty may, however, provide for different exceptions. For instance,

Article 10, para. 5; Egypt–Sweden BIT (1978), Article 8; Romania–Sri Lanka BIT (1981), Article 7, para. 2; Denmark–Romania BIT (1994), Article 4, para. 2.

[58]Pohl et al. (2012), p. 14.

[59]Switzerland-Jamaica BIT (1990), Article 9, paras. 4–5.

[60]Albania-Lithuania BIT (2007), Article 8, para. 2. The exhaustion of local remedies rule has been proposed in the context of discussions during the negotiations of the TTIP between the U.S. and the EU. See Porterfield (2015), pp. 1–12. In 2011, the European Parliament adopted a resolution on the EU's international investment policy that stated that "changes must be made to the present [investor-state] dispute settlement regime", including recognizing "the obligation to exhaust local judicial remedies where they are reliable enough to guarantee due process". See European Parliament, Resolution of 6 April 2011 on the Future European International Investment Policy (2010/2203(INI)), P7_TA (2011)0141, para. 31.

[61]See India-Belarus BIT (2018), Article 15, para. 2; The India-Taipei Association in Taipei and the Taipei Economic and Cultural Center in India BIT (2018), Article 15, para. 4(b).

[62]India Model BIT (2015), Article 15, para. 2. Commentators have interpreted the clause to mean that "the investor must wait for at least five years even if judicial remedies are exhausted earlier" and suggest that "[t]he underlying rationale for the five-year period might be that the Indian judiciary is heavily backlogged and operates slowly and a five-year period is therefore reasonable in the Indian context". See Hanessian and Duggal (2017), p. 222. The Indian Model BIT also provides a clarification whereby "the investor shall not assert that the obligation to exhaust local remedies does not apply or has been met on the basis that the claim under this Treaty is by a different party or in respect of a different cause of action". See India Model BIT (2015), commentary to Article 15, para. 1. As noted by commentators, this language is likely inspired by the desire to avoid certain outcomes linked to a strict application of the "triple identity test" in the context of *fork-in-the-road* clauses. See Hanessian and Duggal (2017), pp. 216–226, footnote 44. However, the Indian Model BIT contains no fork-in-the-road clause and, in fact, the exhaustion requirement is conceptually antithetical to the fork-in-the-road as the former mandates prior recourse to domestic courts rather than offering a choice of forum. Thus, the rationale of the clause likely is to prevent investors from "resorting to technicalities and to reduce the arbitral discretion". See Ranjan and Anand (2017), p. 50. See also the doubts expressed by Hepburn (2009).

[63]For the exceptions to the exhaustion of local remedies, see the discussion in the commentary of the International Law Commission (2006), *Draft Articles on Diplomatic Protection with*

the Indian Model BIT sets forth that domestic remedies need not be exhausted "if the investor or the locally established enterprise can demonstrate that there are no available domestic legal remedies capable of reasonably providing any relief in respect of the same measure or similar factual matters for which a breach of this Treaty is claimed".[64] This has been read as giving "effect to the 'futility' exception to the exhaustion of local remedies in international law in a limited sense".[65]

Certain IIAs require exhaustion of local remedies for breaches of some but not other substantive standards. For instance, the Australia-Hungary BIT and the Australia-Poland BIT specify that the investor need not exhaust local remedies before submitting claims of expropriation and nationalization to international arbitration. However, for disputes in relation to other substantive standards of protection, local remedies must be exhausted first.[66] **96**

A second group of treaties expressly waive the exhaustion rule. Such waiver is for instance included in BITs concluded by Austria,[67] the Belgium–Luxembourg Economic Union,[68] as well as Central and Eastern European States, such as Armenia, Bulgaria, Czech Republic, Croatia, Moldova, Montenegro and Serbia.[69] By specifying that exhaustion does not apply, States remove any uncertainty especially for **97**

---

commentaries, Report of the Fifty-Eighth Session, UN Doc. A/61/10, 2006/II(2) ILC Yearbook, Commentary to Article 15. See also *Swissborough Diamond Mines (Pty) Limited and others v. Kingdom of Lesotho*, PCA Case No. 2013-29, Judgment of the Singapore Court of Appeal, 27 November 2018, paras. 211–222, holding that the only remedies that need to be exhausted are those that are "reasonably available" and that offer a "reasonable possibility of providing effective redress". The Court of Appeal saw no reason for adopting the "less formalistic" approach that prevails in the practice of the European Court of Human Rights, which focuses on whether there is a "reasonable prospect of success". In *Swissborough*, the applicable treaty, the South African Development Community (SADC) (1992) 32 ILM 116, contained an exhaustion of remedies requirement in the following terms: "Disputes between an investor and a State Party concerning an obligation of the latter in relation to an admitted investment of the former, which have not been amicably settled, and after exhausting local remedies shall, after a period of six (6) months from written notification of a claim, be submitted to international arbitration if either party to the dispute so wishes." See Article 28, para. 1 of Annex 1 to the Protocol on Finance and Investment (2006) of the SADC.

[64]India Model BIT (2015), Article 15, para.1, third sub-paragraph.

[65]Hanessian and Duggal (2017), p. 222.

[66]Australia–Hungary BIT (1991), Article 12; Australia-Poland BIT (1991), Article 13. Similarly, the Poland-United Arab Emirates BIT conditions access to investment arbitration to the exhaustion of local remedies in respect of all claims, except those of expropriation and transfers. See Poland-United Arab Emirates BIT (1993), Article 9, para. 2.

[67]Austria–Malaysia BIT (1985), Article 9, para. 2; Austria–Tajikistan BIT (2010), Article 15, para. 2.

[68]Belgium–Indonesia BIT (1970), Article 10; Belgium–Luxembourg Economic Union–Montenegro BIT (2010), Article 12, para. 2; Belgium – Luxembourg Economic Union–Cuba BIT (1998), Article 9, para. 2; Belgium–Luxembourg Economic Union–Burundi BIT (1989), Article 8, para. 3.

[69]Croatia–Jordan BIT (1999), Article 10, para. 2(b); Armenia–Netherlands BIT (2005), Article 9, para. 2; Moldovia–Montenegro BIT (2014) (not in force), Article 8, para. 2(b); Bulgaria–Czech Republic BIT (1999), Article 9, para. 4.

any non-ICSID arbitration options included in the treaty, for which Article 26 of the ICSID Convention would not be applicable.[70]

98 Finally, the vast majority of treaties are silent on whether domestic remedies need to be exhausted before resort to international arbitration.[71] Amongst those are the majority of Swiss BITs.[72]

99 Where the IIA is silent on exhaustion and provides for ICSID arbitration, tribunals have had no difficulty in finding that the customary international law rule on exhaustion does not apply as a consequence of Article 26 of the ICSID Convention.[73] Within the non-ICSID context, investment tribunals under the ASEAN,[74] NAFTA Chapter 11,[75] the ECT,[76] the UNCITRAL Rules[77] and the SCC Rules,[78] have held that exhaustion of local remedies is not a condition for bringing an

[70]See, e.g., Austria-Slovenia BIT (2001), Article 11, para. 3 providing for various arbitration options, including ICSID, ICC, and UNCITRAL arbitration, and specifying that "[e]ach Contracting Party hereby consents unconditionally to the submission of an investment dispute to international conciliation or arbitration. This consent implies the renunciation of the requirement that the internal administrative or judicial remedies should be exhausted".

[71]Brauch (2017), p. 7.

[72]See Johnson (2015), p. 14.

[73]See *Lanco International Inc. v. Argentine Republic*, ICSID Case No. ARB/97/6, Preliminary Decision on Jurisdiction, 8 December 1998, paras. 37–39; *Generation Ukraine, Inc. v. Ukraine*, ICSID Case No. ARB/00/9, Award, 16 September 2003, paras. 13.4–13.5; *EDF International S.A., SAUR International S.A. and León Participaciones Argentinas S.A. v. Argentine Republic*, ICSID Case No. ARB/03/23, Award, 11 June 2012, paras. 1126–1127; *Mr. Franck Charles Arif v. Republic of Moldova*, ICSID Case No. ARB/11/23, Award, 8 April 2013, para. 151; *Helnan International Hotels A/S v. Egypt*, Decision on Annulment, 14 June 2010, paras. 43–47; *Amco v. Indonesia*, Decision on Annulment, 16 May 1986, 1 ICSID Reports 509, para. 63; *IBM v. Ecuador*, Decision on Jurisdiction, 22 December 2003, 13 ICSID Reports 105, para. 80; *AES v. Argentina*, Decision on Jurisdiction, 26 April 2005, 12 ICSID Reports 312, paras. 69-70; *Saipem S.p.A. v. The People's Republic of Bangladesh*, Decision on Jurisdiction, 21 March 2007, paras. 175; Award, 30 June 2009, paras. 174–184; *Emilio Agustin Maffezini v. The Kingdom of Spain*, ICSID Case No. ARB/97/7, Decision on Objections to Jurisdiction, 25 January 2000, paras. 22–23.

[74]*Yaung Chi Oo Trading Pte. Ltd. v. Government of the Union of Myanmar*, ASEAN I.D. Case No. ARB/01/1, Award, 31 March 2003, para. 40.

[75]*Waste Management v. The United Mexican States (No. 2)*, ICSID Case No. ARB(AF)/00/3, Award, 30 April 2004, paras. 116, 133; *Waste Management v. The United Mexican States (No. 2)*, ICSID Case No ARB(AF)/00/3, Decision on Mexico's Preliminary Objection, 26 June 2002, para. 30. See also *William Ralph Clayton and others v. Government of Canada*, PCA Case No. 2009-04, Judgment of the Federal Court of Canada, 2 May 2018, para. 191 (observing that "the prevailing view appears to be that Article 1121 of Chapter Eleven of NAFTA tacitly waives the requirement that litigants must exhaust local remedies before accessing the Chapter Eleven NAFTA arbitration process").

[76]*Nykomb Synergetics Technology Holding AB v. The Republic of Latvia*, SCC, Award, 16 December 2003, 11 ICSID Reports 158, sec. 2.4.

[77]*CME Czech Republic B.V. v. Czech Republic*, UNCITRAL, Final Award, 14 March 2003, paras. 412–413; *Mytilineos Holdings SA v. the State Union of Serbia & Montenegro and the Republic of Serbia*, UNCITRAL, Partial Award on Jurisdiction, 8 September 2006, paras. 220–222.

[78]*RosinvestCo UK v. Russian Federation*, SCC, Award on Jurisdiction, 1 October 2007, para. 153.

investment claim, unless the treaty provides otherwise. This means that in investment arbitration, no matter what arbitration rules govern the proceedings, the customary international rule on exhaustion of local remedies is reversed: the traditional "applicable unless expressly waived" is replaced with "waived unless required".[79] Several reasons are given in support of this proposition.

First, as seen above, many IIAs include a fork-in-the-road provision or require a prior waiver of all domestic proceedings as a condition to access investor-State arbitration. These provisions have the effect opposite to the exhaustion of local remedies rule. The choice-of-forum requirements can only be enforced if read as an implied waiver of the local remedies rule.[80] **100**

Second, it is said that one objective of entering into an arbitration agreement is to re-allocate jurisdiction over a dispute from the local courts to the arbitral tribunal. Hence, unless expressly agreed otherwise, an arbitration agreement should not be read as requiring prior resolution in the courts.[81] **101**

Finally, investment arbitration was established as a system of direct access for investors to international adjudication alternative to diplomatic protection.[82] Therefore, some argue that the diplomatic protection principles developed for the invocation of responsibility by a State should not apply to the prosecution of claims by private parties.[83] **102**

Providing greater scope for the exhaustion of local remedies rule in IIAs in investment arbitration has both supporters and detractors. Those who advocate for a more meaningful role of local remedies before resort to international arbitration argue that the exhaustion requirement would strengthen the rule of law in the host States.[84] Along the same lines, it is said that the fostering of well-functioning judicial institutions in host States "may ultimately help to remedy some of the host-State institutional deficiencies which [investment arbitration was] designed to address",[85] whereas removing investment disputes from the domestic courts discourages local courts from improving the quality of domestic adjudication,[86] and prevents them "from deciding increasingly important matters".[87] Furthermore, deferring an investor-State claim until after domestic courts have resolved the dispute may **103**

[79]Douglas (2012), pp. 98–99; Sornarajah (2010), p. 221; Crawford (2008), p. 352; Schreuer (2010), pp. 72–73; Muchlinski (2009), p. 345.

[80]*Mytilineos Holdings SA v. The State Union of Serbia & Montenegro and Republic of Serbia*, UNCITRAL, Partial Award on Jurisdiction, 8 September 2006, paras. 220–221; Puig (2013), pp. 214–215.

[81]Douglas (2012), p. 98.

[82]See supra at Chap. 2.

[83]Douglas (2004), p. 189; Douglas (2012), pp. 94–96.

[84]Porterfield (2015), p. 5.

[85]UNCTAD (2015), World Investment Report 2015—Reforming International Investment Governance, p. 149 available at https://unctad.org/en/PublicationsLibrary/wir2015_en.pdf.

[86]Ginsburg (2005), pp. 118–119.

[87]Fix-Fierro and López-Ayllón (1997), p. 797.

allow the arbitrator to "benefit from the courts' characterization of the relevant domestic law",[88] in particular, the existence and scope of the property rights.

104 On the other hand, requiring investors to pursue domestic remedies has been criticized for causing delay and increasing costs,[89] especially since in many States it can take several years and layers of judicial review to reach a final judgment. According to some, insisting on exhaustion of local remedies would also carry disadvantages for the host State, as "[p]ublic proceedings in the domestic courts are likely to exacerbate the dispute and may affect the host State's investment climate".[90] Furthermore, "once the host State's highest court has made a decision, it may be more difficult for the government to accept a compromise or a contrary international judicial decision".[91] The very idea that an investment tribunal has authority to review the decision of the host State's highest court may indeed lie uneasy with a number of States.

3.2.3.2 Domestic Litigation Requirements Short of Exhaustion

105 A minority of BITs[92] "soften" the exhaustion of local remedies rule by subjecting it to a time limit.[93] In other words, instead of being required to "exhaust" local remedies, the investor must pursue domestic proceedings for a specified period before it may initiate investor-State arbitration.[94] For the purposes of the domestic litigation requirement, local remedies may include domestic arbitration.[95]

106 A few Swiss BITs with Latin American States include a prior domestic litigation requirement, with some variants from one BIT to the other. The BIT with Argentina requires investors to attempt to settle the dispute before domestic courts for a period of 18 months. If the competent courts do not issue a final judgment ("*jugement de dernière instance*") within such time period, the investor is entitled to start arbitration proceedings.[96] The Swiss BIT with Peru also provides a domestic litigation requirement before arbitration proceedings can be started, and specifies that the investor may commence proceedings if "after a period of 18 months there is no decision on the subject matter by the competent national court, or if, existing such a decision, a party to the dispute takes the view that it infringes a provision of [the

[88] Porterfield (2015), p. 6.

[89] Tietje and Baetens (2014), p. 95.

[90] Schreuer (2010), p. 73.

[91] Schreuer (2010), p. 73.

[92] Pohl et al. (2012), p. 13. See also Schreuer (2010), p. 74.

[93] See for example, Switzerland-Uruguay BIT (1988), Article 10, para. 2; Convention concerning the Reciprocal Encouragement and Protection of Investments, Belgo–Luxembourg Economic Union–Rwanda (1983), Article 10, paras. 3–4; Jordan–Romania BIT (1992), Article 8, paras. 3–4.

[94] Ortiz et al. (2016), p. 334.

[95] United Arab Emirates-Bangladesh BIT (2011) (not in force), Article 9, para. 3.

[96] Switzerland-Argentina BIT (1991), Article 9.

BIT]".[97] The BITs with Chile and Paraguay are somewhat different in that they offer a choice of forum between domestic courts and investment arbitration, without obliging the investor to pursue the one before the other. However, if the investor has opted for domestic courts, it may commence arbitral proceedings "only if after a period of 18 months there is no decision on the subject matter by the competent national court".[98]

Similar variations can be observed in BITs entered into by other countries.[99] The time period during which the investor is required to pursue domestic remedies varies from 3 months[100] to several years.[101] Commonly, the investor is required to pursue domestic proceedings for 18 months.[102] Some BITs require pursuit of local remedies without a precise time limitation.[103] **107**

Arbitral tribunals have applied prior domestic litigation requirements on a number of occasions. Where the investor had started arbitration proceedings without complying with the domestic litigation requirement under the treaty, tribunals have taken different views as to whether the investor could dispense with this requirement in circumstances where domestic remedies would have been futile or would not have allowed a decision to be reached within the prescribed time limit.[104] **108**

---

[97] Switzerland-Peru BIT (1991), Article 9, para. 3.

[98] Switzerland-Chile BIT (1999), Article 9, para. 3. See also Switzerland-Paraguay BIT (1992), Article 9, para. 3.

[99] See, e.g., Korea-Indonesia BIT (2000), Article 9, para. 2 (entitling the investor to submit the dispute to international arbitration if the "dispute cannot be settled within twelve months between the parties to the dispute through pursuit of local remedies"); U.K.-Argentina BIT (1990), Article 8, para. 2(a) (entitling the investor to submit the dispute to international arbitration if the courts have failed to issue a decision within 18 months or, where the decision has been made, but "the Parties are still in dispute"); U.K.-Uruguay BIT (1991), Article 8, para. 2(a) (entitling the investor to submit the dispute to international arbitration if the courts have failed to issue a final decision within 18 months or where the decision is "manifestly unjust or violates the provisions of this Agreement"); Spain-Uruguay BIT (1992), Article XI, para. 3(a) (providing that the dispute may be submitted to international arbitration "if no decision has been taken on the matter 18 months from the initiation of the judicial proceedings [...], or if such a decision exists but the dispute continues between the parties because one of them considers that the said decision is manifestly unjust or contravenes the provisions of this Agreement or any other norm of international law").

[100] See, e.g., Egypt-U.K. BIT (1975), Article 8, para. 1.

[101] As mentioned above, the Indian Model BIT provides for a 5-year period.

[102] See Pohl et al. (2012), p. 14.

[103] See, e.g., Netherlands-United Arab Emirates BIT (2013), Article 9, para. 3 (providing that "[i]n case of a legal dispute concerning an investment in the territory of the United Arab Emirates, the dispute may only be referred to ICSID if the national, party to the dispute, has first submitted the dispute to the competent court of the United Arab Emirates and the dispute has not been settled to the satisfaction of the national").

[104] Compare, e.g., *BG Group Plc. v. The Republic of Argentina*, UNCITRAL, Final Award, 24 December 2007, paras. 140–156; *Ambiente Ufficio S.p.A. v. Argentine Republic*, ICSID Case No. ARB/08/9, Decision on Jurisdiction and Admissibility, 8 February 2013, para. 620; *ICS Inspection and Control Services Limited v. The Argentine Republic*, PCA Case No. 2010-9, Award on Jurisdiction, 10 February 2012, paras. 265, 269, 273; *Giovanni Alemanni and Others v. The Argentine Republic*, ICSID Case No. ARB/07/8, Decision on Jurisdiction and Admissibility,

109 The rationale for the prior domestic litigation requirement is similar to the one underlying the exhaustion of local remedies rule, in that it is aimed at giving the host State an opportunity to redress the wrongful act internally before the dispute is elevated internationally. However, prior domestic litigation requirements have also attracted criticism. For instance, in *Plama v. Bulgaria,* the tribunal described the requirement to undertake a reasonable effort in domestic courts as "nonsensical from a practical point of view".[105] Critics of domestic litigation requirements have argued that the established timeframe is normally too short to enable a meaningful outcome before the local courts.[106] Therefore, for the investor, compliance with this requirement is a mere formality that increases the cost and the duration of the dispute settlement.[107]

110 By contrast, others contend that "[r]estoring a local remedies rule that includes a reasonable, but strict time-frame for those remedies to ensue, [...] while still maintaining a right for an individual to bring a claim directly should those remedies fail, has the potential to balance the rights of investors against the rights of state parties".[108]

3.2.3.3 Resort to Local Remedies as a Possible Element of Substantive Standards

111 Resort to local remedies as discussed in the previous two sub-sections is a condition to the jurisdiction of an arbitral tribunal or the admissibility of the claims. It should be distinguished from the situations in which resort to domestic proceedings by a claimant investor has been found to be a condition for the violation of a substantive standard of protection.[109] This point is addressed briefly here for the sake of completeness.

---

17 November 2014, paras. 315-316; *Philip Morris Brands Sàrl v. Oriental Republic of Uruguay*, ICSID Case No. ARB/10/7, Decision on Jurisdiction, 2 July 2013, paras. 144–148; *Abaclat and Others (Case formerly known as Giovanna a Beccara and Others) v. Argentine Republic*, ICSID Case No. ARB/07/5, Decision on Jurisdiction and Admissibility, 4 August 2011, para. 590; *Urbaser S.A. and Consorcio de Aguas Bilbao Bizkaia, Bilbao Biskaia Ur Partzuergoa v. The Argentine Republic*, ICSID Case No. ARB/07/26, Decision on Jurisdiction, 19 December 2012, paras. 194 and 202; *TSA Spectrum de Argentina S.A. v. Argentine Republic*, ICSID Case No. ARB/05/5, Award, 19 December 2008, paras.108–112; *İçkale İnşaat Limited Şirketi v. Turkmenistan*, ICSID Case No. ARB/10/24, Award, 8 March 2016, para. 260.

[105] *Plama Consortium Limited v. Republic of Bulgaria*, ICSID Case No. ARB/03/24, Decision on Jurisdiction, 8 February 2005, para. 224.

[106] Schreuer (2005), pp. 4–5.

[107] Schreuer (2010), p. 74.

[108] Bjorklund (2004), p. 286.

[109] See generally Kriebaum (2009), pp. 417–462; Spiermann (2009), pp. 463–489; Demirkol (2018), pp. 75–113.

There is consensus that exhaustion of local remedies is a required substantive element of a claim for denial of justice.[110] Beyond denial of justice claims, certain arbitral tribunals have required the claimant investor to resort to local courts to establish violations of other standards of protection. In a number of cases, this requirement has been used to preclude claims for indirect expropriation.[111] In its analysis on expropriation, the tribunal in *Generation Ukraine*, for instance, observed that: **112**

> [. . .] it is not enough for an investor to seize upon an act of maladministration, no matter how low the level of the relevant governmental authority; to abandon his investment without any effort at overturning the administrative fault; and thus to claim an international delict on the theory that there had been an uncompensated virtual expropriation. In such instances, an international tribunal may deem that the failure to seek redress from national authorities disqualifies the international claim, not because there is a requirement of exhaustion of local remedies but because the very reality of conduct tantamount to expropriation is doubtful in the absence of a *reasonable* – not necessarily exhaustive - effort by the investor to obtain correction.[112]

Certain tribunals have also found resort to local remedies relevant for the analysis under the fair and equitable treatment (FET) and full protection and security standards.[113] In those decisions, the investor was required to show that the host State through its whole process of State function,[114] rather than isolated acts, had unfairly denied the investor its right to a properly functioning system presenting adequate remedies.[115] **113**

[110] *Jan de Nul N.V. and Dredging International N.V. v. Republic of Egypt*, ICSID Case No. ARB/04/13, Award, 6 November 2008, paras. 255–261; *Chevron Corporation and Texaco Petroleum Corporation v. The Republic of Ecuador*, UNCITRAL, PCA Case No. 2009-23, Interim Award, 1 December 2008, paras. 235–238. See also Paulsson (2005), pp. 107–112. See also *infra* at Sect. 3.4.1.

[111] *Generation Ukraine v. Ukraine*, ICSID Case No ARB/00/9, Award, 16 September 2003, para. 20.33.

[112] *Generation Ukraine v. Ukraine*, ICSID Case No ARB/00/9, Award, 16 September 2003, para. 20.30.

[113] *Waste Management v. The United Mexican States (No. 2)*, ICSID Case No ARB(AF)/00/3, Award, 30 April 2004, para. 116; *Loewen Group, Inc and Raymond L Loewen v. United States of America*, ICSID Case No ARB(AF)/98/3, Award, 26 June 2003, paras. 154–156.

[114] *GAMI Investments, Inc. v. The Government of the United Mexican States*, UNCITRAL, Final Award, 15 November 2004, para. 103.

[115] *Parkerings-Compagniet AS v. Republic of Lithuania*, ICSID Case No ARB/05/8, Award, 11 September 2007, paras. 318-319; *Waste Management v. The United Mexican States (No. 2)*, ICSID Case No ARB(AF)/00/3, Award, 30 April 2004, para. 115; *Frontier Petroleum Services v. The Czech Republic*, UNCITRAL, Final Award, 12 November 2010, para. 410; *Anatolie Stati, Gabriel Stati, Ascom Group S.A. & Terra Raf Trans Trading v. Republic of Kazakhstan*, SCC Arbitration V (116/2010), Award, 19 December 2013, para. 1092; *Burlington Resources Inc. v. Republic of Ecuador*, ICSID Case No ARB/08/5, Decision on Liability, 14 December 2012, para. 253.

114 Other tribunals have taken a different view and have not required resort to local remedies as a substantive element of alleged breaches other than denial of justice.[116] Certain commentators have also been critical of the suggestion that violation of substantive international standards has occurred only after redress has been sought through the local courts.[117] The annulment committee in *Helnan v. Egypt* set aside the holding from the investment tribunal "which, while disclaiming a requirement of exhaustion of local remedies before ICSID arbitral recourse may be implemented, nevertheless accepts that challenge by [the claimant] of the decision to terminate its [contract] in competent Egyptian administrative courts was required in order to demonstrate the substantive validity of its claims".[118] In so doing, it explained that:

> A single aberrant decision of a low-level official is unlikely to breach the standard unless the investor can demonstrate that it was part of a pattern of state conduct applicable to the case or that the investor took steps within the administration to achieve redress and was rebuffed in a way which compounded, rather than cured, the unfair treatment.
>
> But it is an entirely different matter to impose upon an investor, as a condition [for an international wrong] a requirement that the decision of a [governmental organ] must in turn be challenged in the local courts.[119]

115 For the annulment committee, imposing an effort in domestic courts for the perfection of a substantive breach would introduce "by the back door that which the [ICSID] Convention expressly excludes by the front door".[120]

---

[116]See, e.g., *Mr. Franck Charles Arif v. Republic of Moldova*, ICSID Case No. ARB/11/23, Award, 8 April 2013, paras. 334, 345 (noting that "there is no general requirement to exhaust local remedies for a treaty claim to exist, unless such a claim is for denial of justice. In a claim for denial of justice, the conduct of the whole judicial system is relevant, while in a claim for expropriation, it is the individual action of an organ of the State that is decisive", internal footnote omitted).

[117]See, in particular, Schreuer (2005), pp. 15–16; Schreuer (2010), p. 76.

[118]*Helnan International Hotels AS v. Arab Republic of Egypt*, Decision of the *ad hoc* Committee, ICSID Case No ARB/ 05/19, IIC 440, 14 June 2010, para. 73(1).

[119]*Helnan International Hotels AS v. Arab Republic of Egypt*, Decision of the *ad hoc* Committee, ICSID Case No ARB/ 05/19, IIC 440, 14 June 2010, paras. 50–51.

[120]*Helnan International Hotels AS v. Arab Republic of Egypt*, Decision of the *ad hoc* Committee, ICSID Case No ARB/ 05/19, IIC 440, 14 June 2010, para. 47. In respect of the "effective means" standard and exhaustion, see *Chevron Corporation and Texaco Petroleum Company v. The Republic of Ecuador*, UNCITRAL (*Chevron v. Ecuador I*), Partial Award on the Merits, 30 March 2010, para. 326 (holding that while the "strict exhaustion of local remedies is not necessary, [...] a claimant is required to make use of all remedies that are available and might have rectified the wrong complained of. Moreover, a high likelihood of success of these remedies is not required in order to expect a claimant to attempt them."); *White Industries Australia Limited v. The Republic of India*, UNCITRAL, Final Award, 30 November 2011, paras. 11.4.10–14 (holding that the claimant had not demonstrated that the respondent had failed to provide effective means for it to enforce its rights because the claimant had failed to show that an appeal, which the parties agreed was available as of right to the claimant, would have been "ineffective or futile").

3.2.4 Conclusive Remarks

In sum, in seeking to coordinate domestic and international arbitration proceedings, IIAs have essentially followed either a sequential or alternative approach. The sequential approach, implying the prior use or even exhaustion of local remedies, postulates the priority of domestic courts and, according to some, perhaps a belief in the greater effectiveness of national courts in resolving disputes or in the desirability of litigation at the international level *after* a judicial process has already been pursued or completed at the national level.[121] However, exhaustion or domestic litigation requirements ultimately leave the door open to investment arbitration. By contrast, the alternative approach starts from the idea that domestic courts and investment arbitration are equivalent (at least in theory), leaves the choice of forum to the claimant-investor once the dispute has arisen, and then provides rules to avoid overlaps between the two proceedings. **116**

In spite of these attempts, the *lex lata* is not always able to capture the complexity of the interactions deriving from the fact that, although identical in substance as well as in economic terms, the dispute before the two fora is often not the "same" in strict legal terms (the parties sometimes and most often the legal basis of the claims being different). Hence, *de lege ferenda* and to the extent that States consider it their policy to discourage multiple proceedings about the same measure, fork-in-the-road and waiver clauses should be phrased more broadly and cater for these situations. **117**

3.3 Domestic Courts in Support and Control of Investor-State Arbitral Tribunals

Once an investor has started or intends to start arbitration proceedings, courts can have important supervisory functions over the arbitration process or, otherwise said, they can support or control the arbitration in multiple ways. In this context, a significant distinction exists between an investment arbitration conducted under the ICSID Convention (herein below, "ICSID arbitration" for brevity) and one conducted under any other rules, such as the ICSID Additional Facility (AF), UNCITRAL, ICC, SCC Rules, and others ("non-ICSID arbitration"). In the case of ICSID arbitration, the Washington Convention establishes a "delocalized" procedural framework,[122] governed exclusively by public international law. In ICSID arbitration, the arbitration law of the seat (or *lex arbitri*) plays no role and national courts have no jurisdiction in aid or control of the arbitration. In other words, the "self-contained" process which States designed under the ICSID Convention is **118**

[121] Shany (2007), p. 28.

[122] See generally Delaume (1983), pp. 784–803; Bernardini (2010), pp. 159–188, para. 7.

geared towards making arbitration independent of domestic courts.[123] This entails that any aspects of the arbitral process (appointment of arbitrators, challenges, annulment, revision, etc.) is addressed within the machinery of the Centre established by the ICSID Convention.

119 By contrast, non-ICSID investor-State arbitrations do not benefit from this "delocalization" and, like international commercial arbitrations, are subject to a national *lex arbitri*. For non-ICSID arbitrations, the role of courts in support and control of investment arbitrations is thus potentially much more significant. Non-ICSID arbitrations seated in Switzerland are governed by Chapter 12 of the Swiss Federal Private International Law Act (PILA)[124] and subject to the jurisdiction of the courts of the seat as *juge d'appui* and of the Swiss Federal Tribunal for annulment actions. They are thus submitted to the same regime as international commercial arbitrations with a seat in Switzerland.

120 As mentioned at the outset of this study (see *supra* in Chap. 1), Switzerland has been traditionally one of the most chosen seats for international arbitration in general, including non-ICSID investment arbitrations, due to, *inter alia*, the country's reputation for neutrality and stability as well as the legislation's and the judiciary's pro-arbitration approach. In the last few years, there has been an increase in Swiss-seated investment treaty arbitrations, a trend which may well continue especially for intra-EU disputes as a result of the uncertainties arising from the judgment by the CJEU in *Achmea*.[125] An increase of Swiss-seated arbitrations means, in turn, a potentially greater involvement of the Swiss Federal Tribunal with investment matters, as can already be observed from the growing number of set aside applications of investment awards brought before the Swiss Federal Tribunal (see *infra* Table 3.1, at Sect. 3.3.4, Annulment proceedings of investment awards).

121 The following sections provide an overview of the situations in which domestic courts may rule on investment arbitration matters.

---

[123]Schreuer et al. (2009), p. 351.

[124]References in this report to Chapter 12 of the PILA are to the provisions in the statute that are currently in force at the time of writing. It should be noted that Chapter 12 PILA is currently undergoing a revision. The legislative process to that end is nearing completion. On 24 October 2018, the Swiss Federal Council published its Draft Bill on the reform of Chapter 12 PILA, accompanied by an Explanatory Report addressed to the Swiss Parliament. See *Message concernant la modification de la loi fédérale sur le droit international privé (Chapitre 12 Arbitrage international)* and *Loi fédérale sur le droit international privé (LDIP) (Projet)*, both published in the Swiss Federal Gazette No. 47 of 27 November 2018, available at https://www.admin.ch/opc/fr/federal-gazette/2018/index_47.html (also available in German and Italian). The Draft Bill is due to be reviewed and debated by both Swiss parliamentary chambers in 2019. See Swiss Parliament, *Loi sur le droit international privé, Chapitre 12: Arbitrage international*, available at https://www.parlament.ch/fr/ratsbetrieb/suche-curia-vista/geschaeft?AffairId=20180076. At the time of writing, it is expected that the revised text of Chapter 12 PILA will be enacted in 2020 and will enter into force in 2021.

[125]See CJEU C-284/16, *Slovak Republic v. Achmea BV*, 6 March 2018.

3.3.1 Enforcement of Arbitration Agreement

In a first type of situation, a party may submit a dispute to a domestic court notwithstanding the existence of an agreement between the parties to submit such dispute to investment arbitration. It is most likely that the defendant in the domestic court proceedings will then raise a defense of lack of jurisdiction on the basis of the arbitration agreement, or *exceptio arbitri*. **122**

In non-ICSID investment arbitrations, domestic courts of State Parties to the New York Convention (NYC)[126] have a duty to decline jurisdiction, in accordance with Article II, para. 3, of the Convention, which provides that "the court of a Contracting State, when seized of an action in a matter in respect of which the parties have made a [valid arbitration] agreement, shall, at the request of one of the parties, refer the parties to arbitration unless it finds that the said agreement is null and void, inoperative or incapable of being performed". Article 7 of the PILA provides for a similar rule.[127] **123**

An analogous result is reached in ICSID arbitrations by operation of the exclusivity rule contained in Article 26 of the ICSID Convention. As explained by George Delaume: **124**

> [...] If a court in a Contracting State [to the ICSID Convention] becomes aware of the fact that a claim before it may call for adjudication under ICSID, the court should refer the parties to ICSID to seek a ruling on the subject. Until such a ruling is made, if the possibility exists that the claim may fall within the jurisdiction of ICSID, the court must stay the proceedings pending proper determination of the issue by ICSID.[128]

Courts of a number of countries, including Swiss courts, have recognized these rules when seized of disputes for which an investment arbitration clause was operative.[129] In *MINE v. Guinea*, for instance, in the context of attachment proceedings of an arbitral award rendered under the aegis of the American Arbitration Association, notwithstanding the parties' agreement to refer their disputes to ICSID arbitration, the Swiss Federal Tribunal acknowledged the exclusivity of ICSID **125**

---

[126] New York Convention of 10 June 1958 on the Recognition and Enforcement of Foreign Arbitral Awards (NYC).

[127] Article 7 of the PILA provides as follows: "[i]f the parties have entered into an arbitration agreement [and one of the parties brings an action before a Swiss court], the court must decline jurisdiction unless: (a) the respondent has proceeded on the merits without raising an objection, (b) the arbitration agreement is null and void, ineffective, or incapable of being performed, (c) the arbitral tribunal cannot be constituted for reasons manifestly attributable to the respondent in the arbitration".

[128] Delaume (1984), p. 68 (footnote omitted), *quoted in* Schreuer et al. (2009), p. 386.

[129] These cases have mainly concerned instances where the basis of consent to ICSID jurisdiction was an arbitration clause in an investment contract. Similar results would, however, be reached, *mutatis mutandis*, where consent is perfected through the investor's acceptance of an arbitration offer contained in an IIA.

proceedings by virtue of Article 26 of the ICSID Convention.[130] In the subsequent proceedings before the Geneva Court of First Instance, the Court also affirmed the exclusive character of consent to ICSID arbitration in the following terms:

> According to the [contract], the parties agreed to submit their differences to ICSID. Proceedings initiated by MINE on 7 May 1984 are now pending before the ICSID Arbitral Tribunal. According to Article 26 of the [ICSID Convention], the consent of the parties to arbitration under the Convention is, unless otherwise agreed, considered as implying a waiver of all other remedies. As Switzerland has ratified the Convention it is now part of Swiss law. It should be recognized that, in referring to this Court, the applicant is not acting in conformity with Article 26 of the Convention. [. . .] Since the request which MINE has filed with the Court is contrary to the exclusive nature of ICSID arbitration as provided in Article 26 of the Washington Convention of 18 March 1965, MINE cannot appear before this Court.[131]

126 The subsequent decision by the Supervisory Authority of the *Office des Poursuites* for the Enforcement of Debts and Bankruptcy of Geneva also relied on Article 26 of the ICSID Convention when rejecting MINE's attempt to maintain the attachments.[132]

127 In other cases, domestic courts were asked to enjoin parties from instituting or continuing ICSID proceedings notwithstanding a *prima facie* valid consent to ICSID arbitration. In those instances, where a *prima facie* valid consent to arbitration exists, it would not be permissible for a court to enjoin a party from pursuing the investment arbitration. In *Attorney-General v. Mobil Oil NZ Ltd*, for instance, the New Zealand Government commenced proceedings in its courts to seek to enjoin the investor from continuing to refer the dispute to ICSID in accordance with the agreement entered

---

[130] See Swiss Federal Tribunal, *Maritime International Nominees Establishment (MINE) v. Republic of Guinea*, decision of 4 December 1985, ASA Bulletin (1987) 26 (excerpts) (where the Swiss Federal Tribunal noted that "[a]ccording to [Article 26] of the Washington Convention, the consent of the parties to arbitration within the framework of this Convention is, unless otherwise agreed, considered to imply waiver of the exercise of any other remedy. It follows that the respondent company, to the extent that it is validly bound by the ICSID arbitration clause, must respect the exclusive nature of that procedure. The respondent company cannot therefore have recourse against the appellant to any other measure of asserting pressure or other remedy [. . .]").

[131] Geneva Court of First Instance, *MINE v. Republic of Guinea*, decision of 13 March 1986, ASA Bulletin (1987), 28 (excerpts).

[132] See Autorité de surveillance des offices de poursuite pour dettes et de faillite, *MINE v. Republic of Guinea*, decision of 7 October 1986, ASA Bulletin (1987), 33 (excerpts); 4 ICSID Report 45 (1997) (excerpts); English translation of French original in 26 ILM (1987) 382. The Belgian courts in the same dispute similarly noted ICSID's exclusive competence and found that the proceedings to obtain a seizure fell within the definition of "remedy" in Article 26 and were hence inadmissible. See *Guinea v. MINE*, Belgium, Court of First Instance, Antwerp, 27 September 1985, 4 ICSID Reports 32. See also Brief for the United States of America as Intervenor and Suggestion of Intent, 20 ILM 1436 (1981) in the same dispute before the U.S. courts (in which the United States stated that "[t]o prevent United States courts from improperly asserting jurisdiction over ICSID cases, and to accord the necessary deference to ICSID's jurisdictional autonomy, the United States submits that a rule of abstention should be followed in U.S. courts" and that "a case brought in a United States court which arguably falls within ICSID's exclusive jurisdiction should be stayed to permit ICSID to resolve whether it has jurisdiction").

into by the parties. The High Court of New Zealand found that under the contract, either party was entitled to refer the dispute to ICSID and stayed the domestic proceedings until the ICSID tribunal had determined its jurisdiction.[133] This being so, domestic courts do not always pay deference to Article 26 of the ICSID Convention in this fashion. For instance, in the dispute between SGS and Pakistan, Pakistan commenced domestic arbitration proceedings in Pakistan pursuant to the dispute settlement clause contained in the contract, while SGS subsequently started ICSID proceedings under the Swiss-Pakistan BIT.[134] Each party then applied to the Pakistani courts for injunctions to restrain the other party from pursuing their chosen arbitration option.[135] The Supreme Court of Pakistan ultimately granted Pakistan's request to proceed with the contract arbitration and "restrain[ed] [SGS] from pursuing or participating in the ICSID arbitration".[136]

It should also be noted that in several instances where a domestic court has been **128** seized by a party in an attempt to circumvent investment arbitration proceedings, investment tribunals have been requested to issue provisional measures to restrain that party from initiating or continuing proceedings in another forum, be they arbitration, civil, criminal, bankruptcy, or enforcement proceedings.[137]

There is abundant practice of arbitral tribunals granting interim relief to enjoin **129** parallel domestic litigation. A study of all the known provisional measures decisions issued by ICSID tribunals between 1972 and 2009 shows that over 50% of those decisions concerned a request to enjoin parties from pursuing parallel domestic proceedings.[138] Provisional measures seeking to restrain a party from commencing or continuing parallel domestic litigation are usually requested by the investor, although in certain cases they have also been sought by the State.[139] In essence, investment tribunals have found justification for the issuance of interim relief (sometimes in the form of an "anti-suit injunction"),[140] in the exclusive remedy rule of Article 26 of the ICSID Convention (where such provision was applicable),

[133]See *Attorney-General v. Mobil Oil NZ Ltd*, New Zealand, High Court, Wellington, 1 July 1987, 2 ICSID Review—Foreign Investment Law Journal 497 (1987).

[134]*SGS Société Générale de Surveillance S.A. v. Pakistan*, ICSID Case No. ARB/01/13, Decision on Jurisdiction, 6 August 2003, paras. 1–2.

[135]*SGS Société Générale de Surveillance S.A. v. Pakistan*, ICSID Case No. ARB/01/13, Decision on Jurisdiction, 6 August 2003, paras. 35–38.

[136]*SGS Société Générale de Surveillance S.A. v. Pakistan*, ICSID Case No. ARB/01/13, Decision on Jurisdiction, 6 August 2003, para. 39.

[137]See generally, Brower and Goodman (1991), pp. 431–461; Kalderimis (2016), pp. 549–575; Gil (2009), pp. 353–602; Kaufmann-Kohler et al. (2018), pp. 647–649.

[138]Gil (2009), p. 540.

[139]See *Atlantic Triton Company Limited v. People's Revolutionary Republic of Guinea*, ICSID Case No. ARB/84/1/, 21 April 1986 and *MINE v. Republic of Guinea*, ICSID Case No. ARB/84/4, 6 January 1988. As Gil notes, both these cases related to attachments by domestic courts. See Gil (2009), p. 544.

[140]I.e., an order that restrains, directly or indirectly, temporarily or permanently, the continuation of proceedings before another tribunal or court.

and/or in the need to protect the tribunal's jurisdiction, the integrity of the arbitration proceedings, or in the prohibition of aggravating the dispute.[141]

130 To limit the discussion to two examples in relation to the court proceedings mentioned above, in the dispute between MINE and Guinea,[142] the ICSID tribunal recommended that MINE terminate any proceedings in connection with the dispute and any attachment and provisional measures pending in national courts.[143] Both the Geneva Court of First Instance and the Geneva Bankruptcy Supervision Authority referred to the provisional measures issued by the ICSID tribunal in their decisions giving precedence to ICSID arbitration based on Article 26 of the ICSID Convention.[144]

131 Regarding concurrent *arbitration* proceedings, in *SGS v. Pakistan*, SGS requested the ICSID arbitral tribunal to recommend "that the Islamabad-based

---

[141]In arbitrations under the UNCITRAL 2010 Rules, Article 26, para. 2(b) allows interim measures to prevent a party from taking action that is likely to cause "prejudice to the arbitral process itself". Certain IIAs, such as NAFTA and the EU-Canada FTA, also specifically mention the purpose of protecting the tribunal's jurisdiction amongst the reasons for interim relief. Thus, according to Article 1134 of the NAFTA, "[a] Tribunal may order an interim measure of protection to preserve the rights of a disputing party, or to ensure that the Tribunal's jurisdiction is made fully effective". See also Agreement between the United States of America, the United Mexican States, and Canada (USMCA), 30 November 2018, Article 14.D.7, para. 9. The U.S. Model BIT (2012), as well as numerous recent treaties concluded by the United States, contain wording similar to the NAFTA provision just quoted. Similar language is also present in Article 8.34 of the EU-Canada Comprehensive Economic and Trade Agreement (CETA). Likewise, Article 3.7, para. 4 of the EU-Singapore Investment Protection Agreement (2018) allows investors to request interim measures before arbitration tribunals in order to preserve their rights and interests as claimants, while vesting the same prerogative in domestic courts if interim relief is sought before the constitution of the tribunal. See also EU-Vietnam Investment Protection Agreement (2019), Article 3.47.

[142]See *supra* para. 125. The *MINE* tribunal was the first ICSID tribunal to grant provisional measures to enjoin parallel domestic proceedings. See Gil (2009), pp. 553–554.

[143]MINE v. Republic of Guinea, ICSID Case No. ARB/84/4, Decision on Provisional Measures, 4 December 1985. For an analysis of Atlantic Triton and MINE, see Friedland (1986), pp. 335–357; see also Parra (1993), pp. 37–44.

[144]See Geneva Court of First Instance, *MINE v. Republic of Guinea*, decision of 13 March 1986, ASA Bulletin (1987), 28 (excerpts) ("The ICSID Arbitral Tribunal itself held that the litigation instituted by MINE in the national courts constitutes a violation of its request for ICSID arbitration and constitutes an 'other remedy' as defined in Article 26 of the Convention. In its decision on provisional measures dated 4 December 1985, the ICSID Arbitral Tribunal recommended to MINE that it withdraw and permanently discontinue all pending litigation in the national courts, as well as dissolve all other provisional measures"); Autorité de surveillance des offices de poursuite pour dettes et de faillite, *MINE v. Republic of Guinea*, decision of 7 October 1986, ASA Bulletin (1987), 33 (excerpts); 4 ICSID Report 45 (1997) (excerpts) ("[...] the [ICSID] Arbitral Tribunal [...] recommended to MINE, in its decision on provisional measures of 4 December 1985, that it should withdraw and permanently discontinue all pending litigation before national courts as well as withdraw all other provisional measures. The competent Authority observes that, in resorting to ICSID arbitration proceedings, MINE waived the ability to request provisional measures against the Republic of Guinea in Switzerland. Therefore MINE is committing a manifest abuse of the law in invoking these ICSID proceedings to attempt to obtain the maintenance of an attachment, which is the typical provisional measure").

arbitration pending between SGS and Pakistan be stayed".[145] Finding that SGS had "a *prima facie* right to seek access to international adjudication under the ICSID Convention",[146] the tribunal considered it its "duty to protect this right".[147] It thus recommended that Pakistan inform all the relevant domestic courts of the current standing of the ICSID arbitration and ensure that no action be taken to hold SGS in contempt of court. In parallel, the tribunal also recommended that local arbitration proceedings be stayed until the tribunal decided on its jurisdiction.[148] By contrast, it rejected a broader request for an injunction refraining Pakistan from commencing or participating in proceedings relating in any manner to the ICSID arbitration. This latter request was deemed to restrain the ordinary exercise of Pakistan's normal process of justice.[149]

These types of incidents of court- and tribunal-issued injunctions display a tangible tension between international tribunals and domestic courts where both adjudicative institutions purport to assert jurisdiction over matters relating to the dispute. If these matters are the merits of the investment dispute and there is a valid (or *prima facie* valid) investor-State arbitration agreement, then the jurisdiction of the investment tribunal should prevail. This is not necessarily correct when the matters at issue are merely ancillary to the dispute, such as provisional or interim relief. Article 26 of the ICSID Convention will, in principle, bar the jurisdiction of domestic courts also in this context.[150] The position in non-ICSID arbitrations will depend on any specific IIA provision, the *lex arbitri*, or the applicable arbitration rules. Be that as it may, the issuance of an antisuit injunction always requires careful balancing of a number of principles at play, including the principle of competence-competence of courts and tribunals, which is a general principle of procedure,[151] and **132**

[145] *SGS Société Générale de Surveillance S.A. v. Islamic Republic of Pakistan*, ICSID Case No. ARB/01/13, Procedural Order No 2, 16 October 2002, 18 ICSID Review—Foreign Investment Law Journal (2003), p. 293.

[146] *SGS Société Générale de Surveillance S.A. v. Islamic Republic of Pakistan*, ICSID Case No. ARB/01/13, Procedural Order No 2, 16 October 2002, 18 ICSID Review—Foreign Investment Law Journal (2003), p. 299.

[147] *SGS Société Générale de Surveillance S.A. v. Islamic Republic of Pakistan*, ICSID Case No. ARB/01/13, Procedural Order No 2, 16 October 2002, 18 ICSID Review—Foreign Investment Law Journal (2003), p. 300.

[148] *SGS Société Générale de Surveillance S.A. v. Islamic Republic of Pakistan*, ICSID Case No. ARB/01/13, Procedural Order No 2, 16 October 2002, 18 ICSID Review—Foreign Investment Law Journal (2003), p. 304.

[149] See *SGS Société Générale de Surveillance S.A. v. Islamic Republic of Pakistan*, ICSID Case No. ARB/01/13, Procedural Order No 2, 16 October 2002, 18 ICSID Review—Foreign Investment Law Journal (2003), p. 301 (where the tribunal held that "[w]e cannot enjoin a State from conducting the normal processes of criminal, administrative and civil justice within its own territory. We cannot, therefore, purport to restrain the ordinary exercise of these processes").

[150] Subject to a different agreement between the parties in their instrument recording their consent to arbitration. See ICSID Arbitration Rules, Rule 39, para. 6. See also *infra* at Sect. 3.3.3.

[151] Nottebohm Case (Liechtenstein v. Guatemala), Preliminary Objections, Judgement of November 18, 1953, I.C.J. Reports 1953, pp. 119–20.

the States' sovereignty to exercise their powers to conduct national proceedings within their territory.[152] The latter is particularly pertinent when the local proceedings which are sought to be enjoined are criminal proceedings.[153]

3.3.2 Assistance with the Arbitral Process (Appointment of Arbitrators, Decision on Challenges, etc.)

133 Difficulties may arise in the course of the arbitration proceedings if, for instance, a party fails to perform certain steps, such as appointing its arbitrator. Due to its insulated nature, ICSID arbitration does not require assistance from the courts. Rather, any difficulties in the course of the proceedings are resolved by the Centre, which may be called upon to assist with the appointment of arbitrators, rule on proposals for disqualification, and the like.

134 In non-ICSID arbitrations which are subject to a national *lex arbitri*, courts have, at least in theory, a greater role to play in these matters. Most national arbitration laws provide that the parties or the arbitral tribunal may request the assistance of the courts in the event of difficulties. Under Swiss law as well as other legal systems (notably, France),[154] the court called upon to act in this capacity is often referred to as *juge d'appui*, emphasizing that the court acts in support of the arbitration.[155] Assistance may be required in connection with the constitution of the arbitral tribunal if a party refuses to appoint an arbitrator or to participate in the appointment of a sole arbitrator, if the two parties cannot agree on a sole arbitrator or if the two party-appointed arbitrators cannot agree on the tribunal's president. Support from the judge at the seat may also be required in respect of resolving a challenge to arbitrators and other types of actions. Swiss law provides for such assistance in Articles 179, para. 2, and 180, para. 3, PILA.

135 In practice, however, courts rarely have to step in to assist disputing parties with the matters just referred to. Most non-ICSID arbitrations are conducted pursuant to institutional (e.g., ICC or SCC) or non-institutional (e.g., UNCITRAL) arbitration rules that entrust either an arbitral institution or another appointing authority with support functions. By submitting to arbitration under those rules, parties agree to resort to that arbitral institution or appointing authority for support. As a result, the rules contained in the arbitration laws of most countries providing for the court's role as *juge d'appui*, which apply only in the absence of party agreement, are not triggered. To give an example, in an investment treaty arbitration conducted under the UNCITRAL Rules, difficulties arising with the constitution of the tribunal and challenges to arbitrators will be resolved by an appointing authority chosen by the

[152]For further discussion, see Kalderimis (2016), pp. 549–575.

[153]See Kaufmann-Kohler et al. (2018), pp. 654–655.

[154]See Article 1505 of the French Code of Civil Procedure.

[155]See Kaufmann-Kohler and Rigozzi (2015), p. 57.

parties or, in the absence of such a choice, designated by the PCA.[156] The PCA's practice in investment cases appears to be to designate individuals as appointing authorities.[157] Although rare in practice, the appointing authority chosen by the parties or designated by the designating authority could in theory also be a domestic court.[158]

In addition to matters concerning the appointment and replacement of arbitrators, the assistance of the courts may be requested whenever a compulsory order is required in connection with the conduct of the proceedings (Article 185 PILA), in particular with respect to the taking of evidence (Article 184, para. 2 PILA), for instance to summon a witness who refuses to appear before the arbitral tribunal or to compel a third party to produce documents (section 1782 of Title 28 of the United States Code). **136**

3.3.3 Provisional Measures Issued by Courts

There may be instances where a party wishes to seek interim relief from domestic courts, for example if the tribunal is not yet constituted or if it is constituted but has no jurisdiction to grant the requested measures, or when a measure is directed at a third party, or a court-ordered measure is deemed more efficient.[159] **137**

---

[156]See, e.g. UNCITRAL Rules (2010), Article 6, para. 2 (providing that "[i]f all parties have not agreed on the choice of an appointing authority within 30 days after a proposal made in accordance with paragraph 1 has been received by all other parties, any party may request the Secretary-General of the PCA to designate the appointing authority"). On the constitution of the tribunal see Article 8, para. 1 (providing that if the parties have agreed that a sole arbitrator is to be appointed but are unable to reach agreement on that sole arbitrator within 30 days, "a sole arbitrator shall, at the request of a party, be appointed by the appointing authority") and Article 9, paras. 1 and 2 (providing that where three arbitrators are to be appointed, "[i]f within 30 days after the receipt of a party's notification of the appointment of an arbitrator the other party has not notified the first party of the arbitrator it has appointed, the first party may request the appointing authority to appoint the second arbitrator" and "[i]f within 30 days after the appointment of the second arbitrator the two arbitrators have not agreed on the choice of the presiding arbitrator, the presiding arbitrator shall be appointed by the appointing authority [. . .]"). On the challenge to an arbitrator, see Article 13, para 4 (providing that "[i]f, within 15 days from the date of the notice of challenge, all parties do not agree to the challenge or the challenged arbitrator does not withdraw, the party making the challenge may elect to pursue it. In that case, within 30 days from the date of the notice of challenge, it shall seek a decision on the challenge by the appointing authority").

[157]See Gaukrodger (2018), paras. 205–222, available at http://www.oecd.org/investment/investment-policy/ISDS-Appointing-Authorities-Arbitration-March-2018.pdf.

[158]For instance, the PCA, acting as the designating authority for the Iran-U.S. Claims Tribunal which operates under a revised version of the UNCITRAL Rules, has designated the president of the Supreme Court of the Netherlands as appointing authority for the Iran-U.S. Claims Tribunals. See Gaukrodger (2018), para. 210 (with further references), available at http://www.oecd.org/investment/investment-policy/ISDS-Appointing-Authorities-Arbitration-March-2018.pdf.

[159]See generally Kaufmann-Kohler et al. (2018), pp. 677–678.

138 In the ICSID context, as already mentioned, Article 26 of the Convention provides that, unless otherwise stated, consent to ICSID arbitration is given to the exclusion of any other remedy.[160] It was initially debated whether this exclusion applied to interim relief which a party would request before domestic courts.[161]

139 In 1984, Arbitration Rule 39, para. 6 (formerly Rule 39, para. 5) was introduced to clarify that, except when otherwise stipulated, the parties waive their right to seek interim measures of protection in domestic courts, whether before or after the institution of the ICSID proceedings. For this rule not to apply, the parties must have stipulated so in the agreement recording their consent, namely in the arbitration clause, be it in a contract,[162] national legislation, or a treaty. An illustration of such a stipulation in an IIA can be found in NAFTA Article 1121.[163] Arbitration Rule 39, para. 6 is a further illustration of the insulated nature of ICSID proceedings.

140 By contrast to the Arbitration Rules for arbitrations under the ICSID Convention, Article 46 of the ICSID AF Arbitration Rules expressly authorizes the parties to request assistance from local courts to obtain interim relief. Article 46, para. 4 specifies that, by doing so, the parties are not infringing upon the agreement to arbitrate or affecting the powers of the arbitral tribunal. This feature is explained by the absence of an insulated mechanism in the AF Rules and the fact that AF arbitration is generally subject to a national legal order.[164] Similarly, in the UNCITRAL context, Article 26, para. 3 of the 1976 Arbitration Rules and Article 26, para. 9 of the 2010 Arbitration Rules allow the parties to seek interim relief from domestic courts. Such action is not seen as a breach or waiver of the agreement to arbitrate.

---

[160] See *supra* paras. 68, 124 *et seq.*

[161] See Parra (1993), pp. 37–38. Some authors suggested that since an ICSID tribunal can only *recommend* measures, "the Contracting States did not intend to deprive national courts of the power to prescribe provisional measures". See Collins (1992-III), p. 99.

[162] For instance, the parties could insert into their contract the language of ICSID Model Clause 14, available on the ICSID website, which reads as follows: "Without prejudice to the power of the Arbitral Tribunal to recommend provisional measures, either party hereto may request any judicial or other authority to order any provisional or conservatory measure, including attachment, prior to the institution of the arbitration proceeding, or during the proceeding, for the preservation of its rights and interests". See *ICSID Model Clauses,* available at http://icsidfiles.worldbank.org/icsid/icsid/staticfiles/model-clauses-en/14.htm.

[163] However, Article 1121 NAFTA (entitled "Conditions Precedent to Submission of a Claim to Arbitration") complements the applicable arbitration rules and limits the nature of the relief sought and the courts from which such relief may be requested. It states that, by consenting to arbitration under Chapter 11, a party (an investor on its own behalf or on behalf of an enterprise) waives its right to resort to domestic courts "except for proceedings for injunctive, declaratory or other extraordinary relief, not involving the payment of damages, before an administrative tribunal or court under the law of the disputing Party".

[164] Parra (1993), p. 40.

3.3.4 Annulment Proceedings

Annulment of awards is another area where there is a remarkable difference between ICSID and non-ICSID arbitration. The ICSID Convention offers its own self-contained system of review of awards, whereby an *ad hoc* annulment committee reviews awards based on the grounds for annulment listed in Article 52 of the Convention. Thus, any role for national courts in the annulment of ICSID awards is excluded by the Convention. 141

Awards rendered in non-ICSID arbitrations, by contrast, are subject to the post-award remedies provided by the law of the seat of the arbitration.[165] Annulment (or set aside or vacatur) is thus the area which perhaps showcases the most important role for domestic courts in respect of non-ICSID arbitrations. National arbitration laws follow a variety of approaches in setting out the grounds upon which an arbitral award can be set aside, the standard of review to be followed by the domestic courts, the number of layers of review (one, two, and in certain States even three instances) and the courts competent to review annulment applications. Generally speaking, a comparative analysis of the most important arbitration laws of the world shows that challenges against arbitral awards may only be brought on the basis of a few, narrowly defined grounds of an essentially procedural nature, which include lack of jurisdiction, irregular constitution of the tribunal and lack of impartiality and independence of its members, breach of due process, and public policy (which is the only ground allowing a limited review of the merits). In other words, annulment is concerned with the integrity of the proceedings and not the correctness of the decision. 142

In Switzerland, non-ICSID arbitral awards can be set aside based on one of the grounds listed in Article 190 of the PILA by the Swiss Federal Tribunal.[166] As a result of the growing importance of Switzerland (in particular, Geneva) as a seat of investment arbitrations, the Swiss Federal Tribunal has been seized with a good number of applications for the set aside of investment awards in the last 20 years. In line with the approach followed in other jurisdictions, the Swiss Federal Tribunal admits challenges against non-ICSID awards rendered in disputes arising under investment treaties, when the conditions set out in Chapter 12 of the PILA are fulfilled and according to Article 77 of the Federal Tribunal Act.[167] 143

Swiss law allows parties to waive their right to seek the annulment of the award, provided the parties lack any territorial connection with Switzerland and the expression of their intent to exclude annulment proceedings meets certain form requirements.[168] According to the Swiss Federal Tribunal, the parties must clearly and 144

---

[165]See generally Hober and Eliasson (2018), pp. 759–796.

[166]On challenges of investment arbitration awards before the Swiss Federal Tribunal, see generally Scherer et al. (2009), pp. 256–279; Radjai and Stirnimann (2013), pp. 1096–1099.

[167]*Loi sur le Tribunal fédéral*, RS 173.110.

[168]See Article 192, para. 1 PILA (providing that "[i]f none of them has its domicile, habitual residence, or a business establishment in Switzerland, the parties may, by an express statement in

unambiguously state their intent to waive the right to challenge the award in accordance with Article 190, para. 2 PILA.[169] In a decision dealing with the award on jurisdiction in *Saluka v. The Czech Republic*, the Swiss Federal Tribunal had an opportunity to discuss an alleged waiver in a BIT, specifically in Article 8, para. 7 of the Dutch-Czech BIT. That provision stipulates that the decision of the arbitral tribunal "shall be final and binding upon the parties to the dispute".[170] In reliance on the interpretation rules in the Vienna Convention on the Law of Treaties ("VCLT") as codification of customary international law because it was not directly applicable, the Court came to the same result as in commercial arbitrations with similar wording and held that the waiver was invalid.[171] It considered that the "final and binding" language did not rule out a remedy such as annulment which was said to be limited to "the most severe defects".[172] It also found support in Article 53, para. 1 of the ICSID Convention, which provides that ICSID awards are "binding on the parties", a characteristic that does not rule out the availability of an annulment mechanism. While it is conceivable that the parties may contractually waive their right to seek annulment of the award in terms that fulfil the form requirements of Article 192, para. 1 of the PILA,[173] IIAs do normally not contain such express language and thus the application of Article 192, para. 1 PILA to non-ICSID investment arbitrations appears limited.

145 Table 3.1 summarizes all the known investment treaty arbitrations for which an action to set aside has been brought before the Swiss Federal Tribunal.[174] None of the cases decided thus far concerned a Swiss BIT (and thus, a Swiss party), which is unsurprising given that the seat is often chosen as a neutral venue between the disputing parties. Thus far, the Swiss Federal Tribunal has never upheld an application to annul an investment award, which is in line with its pro-arbitration attitude.

---

the arbitration agreement or by a subsequent written agreement, exclude any action for annulment in full or limit it to one or the other of the grounds listed in Article 190(2)"). On the waiver of annulment under Swiss law, see generally Kaufmann-Kohler and Rigozzi (2015), pp. 437–447.

[169] Kaufmann-Kohler and Rigozzi (2015), p. 439 (with further references).

[170] Netherlands-Czech Republic BIT (1991), Article 8, para. 7.

[171] Swiss Federal Tribunal decision, *Czech Republic v. Saluka Investments BV*, decision of 7 September 2006, 4P.114/2006, para. 5.4, ASA Bulletin (2007), 123, 139–143.

[172] Swiss Federal Tribunal decision, *Czech Republic v. Saluka Investments BV*, decision of 7 September 2006, 4P.114/2006, para. 5.4.2.1, ASA Bulletin (2007), 123, 140–141.

[173] See, for instance, Swiss Federal Tribunal, *Lebanon v. France Télécom*, decision of 10 November 2005, 4P.98/2005, ASA Bulletin (2006), 98, para. 4 (where the parties had concluded an agreement in which they, *inter alia*, consolidated two pending arbitration proceedings, the first under a contract, and the second under the BIT. Such agreement contained a waiver to challenge the jurisdiction of the arbitral tribunal, which the Swiss Federal Tribunal found to constitute a valid waiver agreement pursuant to Article 190, para. 2 of the PILA).

[174] In addition to the annulment cases set out in Table 3.1, the Swiss Federal Tribunal was also seized with a request for revision of an investment treaty award. See Swiss Federal Tribunal, *Walter Bau AG (in liquidation) v. The Kingdom of Thailand*, decision of 23 July 2012, 4A_570/2011, available at http://www.swissarbitrationdecisions.com.

Table 3.1 Annulment proceedings of investment awards before the Swiss Federal Tribunal (*Tribunal Fédéral* or "TF")

Date of TF decision	TF case number	Parties	Arbitration rules/ Institution	Seat of arbitration	IIA	Language of TF proceedings	Grounds invoked	Application successful?
20 September 2000	1P.113/ 2000	*Applicant*: Republic of Poland *Respondent*: Saar Papier Vertriebs GmbH (Germany)	UNCITRAL (ad hoc)	Zurich	Germany-Poland BIT (1989)	German	PILA Article 190, para. 2(b) (*res iudicata*—the matter had been already decided with final award of 16 October 1995)	No
1 March 2002	4P.200/ 2001	*Applicant*: Saar Papier Vertriebs GmbH (Germany) *Respondent*: Republic of Poland	UNCITRAL (ad hoc)	Zurich	Germany-Poland BIT (1989)	German	PILA Article 190, para. 2(b) (Tribunal expanded matter in dispute) PILA Article 190, para. 2(c) (amount indicated in award did not correspond to claimed amount) PILA Article 190, para. 2(d) (request for hearing rejected, Tribunal did not accept all evidence) PILA Article 190, para. 2(e) (Tribunal's definition of "damages" violates prohibition of expropriation without compensation)	No

(continued)

Table 3.1 (continued)

Date of TF decision	TF case number	Parties	Arbitration rules/ Institution	Seat of arbitration	IIA	Language of TF proceedings	Grounds invoked	Application successful?
10 November 2005	4P.98/ 2005	*Applicant*: Republic of Lebanon *Respondents*: France Telecom Mobile International (FTMI) (France) & Telecom Mobile Lebanon (FTML) (Lebanon)	UNCITRAL (ad hoc)	Geneva	France-Lebanon BIT (1996)	French	PILA Article 190, para. 2(b) (Tribunal wrongly upheld jurisdiction—appeal on this point declared inadmissible pursuant to Article 192, para. 1) PILA Article 190, para. 2(e) (Tribunal did not take into account *res judicata* of recovery order and violation of principle of *pacta sunt servanda*)	No
10 November 2005	4P.154/ 2005	*Applicant*: Republic of Lebanon *Respondents*: France Telecom Mobile International (FTMI) (France); Telecom Mobile Lebanon (FTML) (Lebanon)	UNCITRAL (ad hoc)	Geneva	France-Lebanon BIT (1996)	French	PILA Article 190, para. 2(a) (Tribunal irregularly constituted—Award not signed by President of Tribunal) PILA Article 190, para. 2(b) (Tribunal inadmissibly modified content of original award through corrective award) PILA Article 190, para. 2(c) (Tribunal modified content of award) PILA Article 190, para. 2(e) (procedural defects inter alia violation of confidentiality and right to be heard)	No

7 September 2006	4P.114/ 2006	*Applicant*: Czech Republic *Respondent*: Saluka Investments B.V.	UNCITRAL (PCA)	Geneva	Czech Republic-Netherlands BIT (1991)	German	PILA Article 190, para. 2(b) (Tribunal had no jurisdiction *ratione temporis*)	No
6 October 2015	4A_34/ 2015	*Applicant*: Republic of Hungary *Respondent*: EDF International S.A.	UNCITRAL (PCA)	Zurich	ECT	French	PILA Article 190, para. 2(b) (no jurisdiction as Applicant had withheld consent to arb. for contract claims) PILA Article 190, para. 2(d) (violation of right to be heard) PILA Article 190, para. 2(e) (violation of principle *pacta sunt servanda*)	No
20 September 2016	4A_616/ 2015	*Applicant*: RECOFI *Respondent*: Viet Nam	UNCITRAL (PCA)	Geneva	France-Viet Nam BIT (1996)	French	PILA Article 190, para. 2(b) (Tribunal misinterpreted the term "investment") PILA Article 190, para. 2(d) (violation of right to be heard)	No
20 July 2017	4A_98/ 2017	*Applicant*: Russian Federation *Respondent*: Yukos Universal Limited (Isle of Man)	UNCITRAL (PCA)	Geneva	ECT	French	PILA Article 190, para. 2(b) (*issue not specified—appeal dismissed as inadmissible*)	No
14 December 2017	4A_157/ 2017	*Applicant*: Republic of Poland *Respondents*: Horthel Systems BV, Poland Gaming Holding BV and Tesa Beheer BV	UNCITRAL (PCA)	Geneva	Netherlands—Poland BIT (1992)	French	PILA Article 190, para. 2(e) (violation of public policy)	No

(continued)

Table 3.1 (continued)

Date of TF decision	TF case number	Parties	Arbitration rules/ Institution	Seat of arbitration	IIA	Language of TF proceedings	Grounds invoked	Application successful?
15 February 2018	4A_507/ 2017	*Applicant*: Republic of Serbia *Respondent*: Mytilineos Holdings SA	UNCITRAL (PCA)	Zurich	Greece-Serbia BIT (1997)	German	*Not specified in TF order*	N/A [appeal withdrawn]
16 October 2018	4A_396/ 2017	*Applicant:* Russian Federation *Respondent:* PJSC Ukrnafta	UNCITRAL (PCA)	Geneva	Ukraine-Russia BIT (1998)	German	PILA Article 190, para. 2(b) (BIT not applica-ble to territory, Respondent was no investor, assets no investment)	No
16 October 2018	4A_398/ 2017	*Applicant:* Russian Federation *Respondent:* Stabil LLC et al.	UNCITRAL (PCA)	Geneva	Ukraine-Russia BIT (1998)	German	PILA Article 190, para. 2(b) (BIT not applica-ble to territory, Respondent was no investor, assets no investment)	No
11 December 2018	4A_65/ 2018	*Applicant:* Republic of India *Respondent:* Deutsche Telekom AG	UNCITRAL (PCA)	Geneva	Germany-India BIT (1995)	French	PILA Article 190, para. 2(b) (BIT does not protect indirect invest-ments and investors or pre-investments; India's conduct fell within the national security exception) PILA Article 190, para. 2(d) (Tribunal refused to consider BIT negotiation history)	No

12 December 2019	4A_244/2019	*Applicant*: Russian Federation *Respondent*: PJSC Ukrnafta	UNCITRAL (PCA)	Geneva	Ukraine-Russia BIT (1998)	German	PILA Article 190 para. 2(e)—investment tainted by fraud/corruption (*ground held to be inadmissible as presented in reliance on evidence not submitted in the arbitration and facts not established in the award*) Award (at least partly) a nullity, or violation of public policy (PILA Article 190 para. 2 (e))—Tribunal decided on a question that was not freely determinable between a Contracting State and a private person, nor arbitrable under PILA Article 177	No
12 December 2019	4A_246/2019	*Applicant*: Russian Federation *Respondent*: Stabil LLC *et al.*	UNCITRAL (PCA)	Geneva	Ukraine-Russia BIT (1998)	German	PILA Article 190 para. 2(e)—investment tainted by fraud/corruption (*ground held to be inadmissible as presented in reliance on evidence not submitted in the arbitration and facts not established in the award*)	No

(continued)

Table 3.1 (continued)

Date of TF decision	TF case number	Parties	Arbitration rules/ Institution	Seat of arbitration	IIA	Language of TF proceedings	Grounds invoked	Application successful?
							Award (at least partly) a nullity, or violation of public policy (PILA Article 190 para. 2 (e))—Tribunal decided on a question that was not freely determinable between a Contracting State and a private person, nor arbitrable under PILA Article 177	

3.3.5 Enforcement

The last situation in which a domestic court may be faced with investment arbitration matters is in connection with a request to enforce an arbitral award.[175] Once again, the role of courts in the enforcement of ICSID and non-ICSID awards must be distinguished. **146**

Pecuniary obligations imposed by awards issued in ICSID arbitrations benefit from a special treatment in the sense that they require no enforcement under the NYC (on which see below). Indeed, pursuant to Article 54, para. 1 of the ICSID Convention, ICSID Contracting States, including Switzerland, are committed to enforce the award "as if it were a final judgment of a court in that State".[176] This means that a domestic court or authority before which execution (as opposed to enforcement) of an ICSID award is sought is restricted to ascertaining the award's authenticity[177] and to any execution requirements and defenses under national law (e.g. the defense of prior payment of the award). This is yet another feature of the "self-contained" ICSID Convention system. **147**

Enforcement of non-ICSID awards is governed by the national law of the State where enforcement is sought and by the NYC. **148**

In Switzerland, one must distinguish between awards rendered in and outside of Switzerland. For the former, the position under Swiss law is quite unique in comparative law terms, given that arbitral awards rendered in Switzerland are assimilated to court judgments without any further formalities.[178] Where the parties have validly waived the right to challenge the award in accordance with Article 192, para. 1 PILA (which is an unlikely scenario in investment treaty arbitration, as observed above), the losing party will be able to rely on the grounds for refusal of **149**

---

[175] See generally Reinisch (2018), pp. 797–822.

[176] Furthermore, Under Article 54, para. 2 ICSID Convention, "[e]ach Contracting State shall notify the Secretary-General of the designation of the competent court or other authority for this purpose and of any subsequent change in such designation". Switzerland has designated different courts for each canton. See Designations of Courts or Other Authorities Competent for the Recognition and Enforcement of Awards Rendered Pursuant to the Convention (Article 54, para. 2 of the Convention), ICSID/8-E, available at https://icsid.worldbank.org/en/Documents/icsiddocs/ICSID%208-Contracting%20States%20and%20Measures%20Taken%20by%20Them%20for%20the%20Purpose%20of%20the%20Convention.pdf.

[177] Schreuer et al. (2009), p. 1148.

[178] Thus, if an award orders the payment of monies, it will be sufficient for the creditor to issue an order to pay in the context of debt collection proceedings and then to obtain the lifting of a possible objection to such order. The debtor will only be able to resist the enforcement of the award by establishing that "the debt has been paid or that its payment has been deferred [after the issuance of the award], or [. . .] that it is time-barred" (Article 81, para. 1 of the Federal Act on Debt Collection and Insolvency (DEBA) of 11 April 1889). It is possible, but not necessary, to obtain a certificate of enforceability of the award (Article 193, para. 2 PILA). When such a certificate has been issued, the court seized with the debt collection proceedings is bound by it and cannot refuse enforcement on the basis of Article 81, para. 1 DEBA. See Kaufmann-Kohler and Rigozzi (2015), p. 415, footnote 355.

enforcement under Article V of the NYC, in accordance with Article 192, para. 2 PILA.

150 On the other hand, enforcement in Switzerland of non-ICSID awards rendered outside of Switzerland is subject to the NYC. By providing that "the recognition and enforcement of foreign arbitral awards are governed by the New York Convention of 10 June 1958 on the recognition and enforcement of foreign arbitral awards" (Article 194 of the PILA), and withdrawing its reciprocity reservation, Switzerland made the recognition and enforcement of *all* awards rendered outside of Switzerland subject to the NYC, even when they were rendered in a country that is not a Contracting State of the NYC.[179]

151 To be enforceable under the NYC, the decision at issue must be an arbitral award within the meaning of the NYC and, in particular, it must be "foreign", i.e. "made in the territory of a State other than the State where the recognition and enforcement [...] are sought" (Article I, para. 1, NYC). From the point of view of Swiss law, an arbitral award is "foreign" if it emanates from a tribunal whose seat was outside Switzerland.[180] There will thus normally be no difficulty for courts in determining that non-ICSID investment awards rendered in arbitration seated abroad fulfil this requirement. For the avoidance of doubts, certain IIAs specify that a disputing party may seek enforcement of an arbitration award rendered on the basis of the IIA "under [...] the New York Convention".[181] Treaties may further stipulate that "[a] claim that is submitted to arbitration under [the IIA] shall be considered to arise out of a commercial relationship or transaction for purposes of Article I of the New York Convention",[182] which specification is made in light of the fact that Article I, para. 3, of the Convention allows States to make a declaration to the effect that they "will apply the Convention only to differences arising out of legal relationships, whether contractual or not, *which are considered as commercial* under the national law of the State making such declaration".[183]

152 In reviewing an investment award under the NYC, domestic courts, including Swiss courts, will be bound by the exclusive grounds for non-recognition and non-enforcement listed in Article V of the Convention. Article V NYC includes

---

[179]See Kaufmann-Kohler and Rigozzi (2015), p. 518. In accordance with Article I, para. 3 NYC, "[w]hen signing, ratifying or acceding to this Convention [...] any State may on the basis of reciprocity declare that it will apply the Convention to the recognition and enforcement of awards made only in the territory of another Contracting State". When it acceded to the NYC in 1965, Switzerland made a reciprocity reservation under this provision. The reservation was withdrawn, with effect as of 23 April 1993 (AS/RO 1993, 2439), upon the entry into force of Chapter 12 PILA (and more specifically of its Article 194). *Ibid,* footnote 615.

[180]Kaufmann-Kohler and Rigozzi (2015), p. 522.

[181]U.S. Model BIT (2012), Article 34, para. 9.

[182]U.S. Model BIT (2012), Article 34, para. 10. See also ECT, Article 26, para. 5(b) providing that "[a]ny arbitration under this Article shall at the request of any party to the dispute be held in a state that is a party to the New York Convention. Claims submitted to arbitration hereunder shall be considered to arise out of a commercial relationship or transaction for the purposes of article I of that Convention."

[183]NYC, Article I, para. 3 (emphasis added).

grounds that relate to the tribunal's jurisdiction, namely the validity of the arbitration agreement, including arbitrability, form, and the parties' capacity to submit to arbitration, as well as grounds covering the fundamental principles of procedure, irregularities in the tribunal's composition, *ultra petita* awards, and public policy.

Finally, domestic courts may be faced with the application of the rules on immunity of States from execution, which are left intact in the enforcement of both non-ICSID and ICSID awards.[184] Issues of immunity often arise when alleged State assets located in Switzerland are attached in order to satisfy the award. **153**

Generally speaking, a Swiss court seized with an application to execute an investment treaty award against sovereign States would grant the application if three requirements are met: (1) the State has not acted as a sovereign ("*iure imperii*") in the legal relationship which underlies the claim giving rise to the award, but has acted as the holder of private rights ("*iure gestionis*"); (2) the assets targeted by the execution measures are not to be assigned to tasks which are part of the foreign State's duty as a public authority, and are thus not excluded from execution proceedings pursuant to Article 92, para. 1 of the Federal Act on Debt Collection and Insolvency (DEBA); and (3) the transaction out of which the claim against the foreign State arises must have a sufficient connection to Switzerland (in German: "*Binnenbeziehung*"; in French "*rattachement suffisant*").[185] **154**

In the ICSID AF case of *Sistem Muhendislik Insaat Sanayi ve Ticaret A.S. v. Kyrgyz Republic*, the claimant sought to attach claims held by the International Air Transport Association (IATA), seated in Geneva, against the respondent State for charges for surveillance of national airspace. In a decision of 2011, the Swiss Federal Tribunal rejected an appeal against the lower court's decision that had refused execution on the grounds that the surveillance of national airspace was a sovereign task, and hence *de iure imperii*. Charges levied for this task were thus exempted from attachments pursuant to Article 92 DEBA.[186] **155**

The Swiss Federal Tribunal's decision of 7 September 2018 concerning the enforcement of an UNCITRAL investment treaty award against Uzbekistan marks a rare instance of the application of the *Binnenbeziehung* doctrine to an investment treaty award.[187] In application of this doctrine, the Swiss Federal Tribunal declined to enforce the award against the Republic of Uzbekistan, on the grounds that the underlying dispute presented no "substantial link" with Switzerland.[188] The Court **156**

[184] In the context of the ICSID Convention, this is expressly provided by Article 55, which stipulates that "[n]othing in Article 54 [on recognition and enforcement of ICSID awards] shall be construed as derogating from the law in force in any Contracting State relating to immunity of that State or of any foreign State from execution".

[185] See generally Giroud (2012), pp. 758–766; Radjai and Stirnimann (2013), pp. 1109–1110.

[186] See Swiss Federal Tribunal, *A. A.S. v. Etat du Kirghizistan, Office des poursuites de Genève*, decision of 23 November 2011, 5A_681/2011, ASA Bulletin (2012), pp. 819–824.

[187] See Swiss Federal Tribunal, *A. Limited v. Republic of Uzbekistan*, decision of 7 September 2018, 5A_942/2017, available at http://www.swissarbitrationdecisions.com.

[188] For the Swiss Federal Tribunal, "a levy of execution against a foreign state is subject to the prerequisite that the legal relationship in question has a sufficient domestic connection with the

considered that the requirement was a "rule of procedure" imposed by Swiss law, and observed that Article III of the NYC makes it clear that "each signatory state permits arbitral awards to be enforced in line with the procedural requirements of the sovereign territory in which enforcement of the arbitral award is being sought".[189] The decision of the Federal Tribunal should be viewed in light of the limited scope of review available to it in the attachment proceedings at issue.[190] Indeed, the Federal Tribunal expressly left open "what findings [it] would reach if it was called to rule upon an appeal from a *res judicata* decision on the recognition and enforcement of a foreign arbitral award made against a foreign state without limiting the power to review".[191] Be that as it may, where enforcement of a foreign award is governed by a treaty such as the NYC, the application of a "substantial link" requirement appears, in the authors' view, incompatible with Switzerland's international obligations under the Convention, which makes no provision for this requirement. Article III NYC deals with procedure in the strict sense of the word and does not allow to add

---

territory of Switzerland. There must be circumstances present that tie the legal relationship so closely to Switzerland that there is a good justification for proceeding before the Swiss authorities against the foreign state [...]. This prerequisite will, in particular, be considered to be met if the obligation from which the disputed attachment claim is derived was established in Switzerland or was to be performed in Switzerland, or if the foreign state has undertaken some acts in Switzerland by which it established Switzerland as the place of performance. However, it is not sufficient that assets of a foreign state are located in Switzerland or that the claim was the subject of an award by an arbitral tribunal with its seat in Switzerland". See Swiss Federal Tribunal, *A. Limited v. Republic of Uzbekistan*, decision of 7 September 2018, 5A_942/2017, para. 6.3.2.

[189]Swiss Federal Tribunal, *A. Limited v. Republic of Uzbekistan*, decision of 7 September 2018, 5A_942/2017, para. 6.3.4. Article III of the NYC provides that: "Each Contracting State shall recognize arbitral awards as binding and enforce them in accordance with the rules of procedure of the territory where the award is relied upon, under the conditions laid down in the following articles. There shall not be imposed substantially more onerous conditions or higher fees or charges on the recognition or enforcement of arbitral awards to which this Convention applies than are imposed on the recognition or enforcement of domestic arbitral awards".

[190]See Swiss Federal Tribunal, *A. Limited v. Republic of Uzbekistan*, decision of 7 September 2018, 5A_942/2017, paras. 2, 4 and 6.4.4 (review is limited to "arbitrariness" and "pursuant to the consistent jurisprudence of the Federal Tribunal, a decision will not be deemed arbitrary merely because another outcome appears arguable or even more correct. Rather, arbitrary application of the law will only be deemed to have occurred where the challenged decision is manifestly untenable and in clear conflict with the facts, or represents a gross violation of a norm or undisputed legal principle, or runs counter to and offends notions of justice; what is required in this respect is that the decision is found to be arbitrary not merely in terms of its reasoning, but also in terms of its outcome"; "The challenged decision is based on the legal view that the requirement of a sufficient domestic connection will also apply in the context of the New York Convention. The Appellant does not succeed in proving that the Cantonal Court has acted in an arbitrary way in assessing the legal situation in this manner").

[191]Swiss Federal Tribunal, *A. Limited v. Republic of Uzbekistan*, decision of 7 September 2018, 5A_942/2017, para. 6.4.4.

requirements (such as the "substantial link" requirement) which ultimately result in expanding the exhaustive list of grounds contained in Article V.[192]

3.4 State Liability: Investment Tribunals Reviewing Domestic Court Conduct

This chapter provides an overview of the main instances in which investment tribunals review the conduct of domestic courts for the purposes of establishing a violation of international law.[193] **157**

A State can be held liable for violations of international law incurred as a result of a decision of a national court. Pursuant to Article 4, para. 1, of the ILC Draft Articles on State Responsibility, courts are organs of the State as are its parliament and the government: **158**

> The conduct of any State organ shall be considered an act of that State under international law, whether the organ exercises legislative, executive, judicial or any other functions, whatever position it holds in the organization of the State, and whatever its character as an organ of the central Government or of a territorial unit of the State.

Thus, in principle, it is possible for investment treaty tribunals to review whether conduct by State courts can violate international law and specifically the treaty standards contained in the IIA. They do so under the main heading of "denial of justice" (*infra* at Sect. 3.4.1) as well as under other treaty guarantees (*infra* at Sect. 3.4.2). One area that has given rise to a number of awards recently deals with court decisions in the field of commercial arbitration (*infra* a Sect. 3.4.3). **159**

3.4.1 Denial of Justice

Typically, domestic court conduct may be reviewed under the "denial of justice" standard, an old institution of customary international law, which is concerned **160**

[192]This being so, U.S. courts, for instance, adopt a similar approach when they add a requirement of personal jurisdiction to entertain the enforcement of a foreign award or dismiss actions to enforce foreign awards on *forum non conveniens* grounds. See *In Re: the Arbitration Between Monegasque De Reassurances SAM (Monde Re), v. Nak Naftogaz of Ukraine and State of Ukraine*, 311 F 3d 488 (2d Cir 2002); *First Inv. Corp. of Marshall Islands v. Fujian Mawei Shipbuilding*, Ltd, 703 F.3d 742, 749-50 (5th Cir. 2012) ("Even though the New York Convention does not list personal jurisdiction as a ground for denying enforcement, the Due Process Clause requires that a court dismiss an action, on motion, over which it has no personal jurisdiction [. . .]. Congress could no more dispense with personal jurisdiction in an action to confirm a foreign arbitral award than it could under any other statute").

[193]For further references, see Paulsson (2005); Douglas (2014), pp. 867–900; Demirkol (2018).

specifically with the conduct of courts. There is general consensus that denial of justice is one of the sub-elements of the FET standard contained in most IIAs.[194]

161 A claim for denial of justice may be asserted only after all available means offered by the State's judiciary have been exhausted. The rationale for requiring exhaustion of remedies as a substantive element of a denial of justice is that as long as the domestic legal system is still reviewing the case (within a reasonable timeframe), justice cannot yet be regarded as denied.[195] Typically, investment tribunals set a demanding test for a showing of denial of justice. So for instance, the ICSID tribunal in *Philip Morris v. Uruguay*:

> As held by one decision, "[a] denial of justice implies the failure of a national system as a whole to satisfy minimum standards." The high standard required for establishing this claim in international law means that it is not enough to have an erroneous decision or an incompetent judicial procedure, arbitral tribunals not being courts of appeal. For a denial of justice to exist under international law there must be "clear evidence of ... an outrageous failure of the judicial system" or a demonstration of "systemic injustice" or that "the impugned decision was clearly improper and discreditable."[196]

162 Thus, investment treaty tribunals do not acts as an additional appeal level reviewing domestic court rulings on the merits.[197] Their function "is not to correct errors of domestic procedural or substantive law which may have been committed by the national courts".[198] To succeed with a claim that the host State courts have denied an investor justice, the investor needs to demonstrate that "the relevant courts refuse[d] to entertain suit, [...] subject[ed] it to undue delay, or [...] administer [ed] justice in a seriously inadequate way".[199] A misapplication of the law will not suffice, unless it can be shown that such misapplication was "clear and malicious".[200]

---

[194] See Demirkol (2018), pp. 33–34 (with further references).

[195] Shany (2007), p. 31.

[196] *Philip Morris Brands Sàrl, Philip Morris Products S.A. and Abal Hermanos S.A. v. Oriental Republic of Uruguay (formerly FTR Holding SA, Philip Morris Products S.A. and Abal Hermanos S.A. v. Oriental Republic of Uruguay)*, ICSID Case No. ARB/10/7, Award, 8 July 2016, paras. 499–500.

[197] The 2015 Indian Model BIT specifies that investor-State arbitral tribunals under the treaty "shall not have the jurisdiction to [...] review the merits of a decision made by a judicial authority of the Parties". See Indian Model BIT (2015), Article 13, para. 5(i).

[198] *Liman Caspian Oil BV and NCL Dutch Investment BV v. Republic of Kazakhstan*, ICSID Case No. ARB/07/14, Excerpts of Award, 22 June 2010, para. 274.

[199] *Robert Azinian, Kenneth Davitian and Ellen Baca v. United Mexican States*, Award, 1 November 2009, para. 102 ("A denial of justice could be pleaded if the relevant courts refuse to entertain a suit, if they subject it to undue delay, or if they administer justice in a seriously inadequate way").

[200] *Robert Azinian, Kenneth Davitian and Ellen Baca v. United Mexican States*, Award, November 2009, para. 103 ("There is a fourth type of denial of justice, namely the clear and malicious misapplication of the law").

3.4.2 *Other International Standards of Protection*

Denial of justice is not the only international law standard that can be breached by domestic courts. IIAs recognize that the State can commit other breaches through its courts that do not amount to denial of justice and for which less stringent criteria apply.[201] For instance, recent treaties concluded by the EU, such as the CETA, specifically recognize that a fundamental breach of due process in judicial proceedings, manifest arbitrariness and targeted discrimination are wrongful acts independent from denial of justice.[202] **163**

Investment tribunals have entertained claims relating to alleged wrongs committed by domestic courts under a number of different IIA standards. Unlike for denial of justice, a breach of other international IIA obligations does not require exhaustion of local remedies,[203] unless expressly provided otherwise. Therefore, even the judicial act of a first instance court may give rise to a treaty breach.[204] **164**

In a number of cases, investment tribunals have found that the FET standard protects investors from wrongful treatment by the judiciary aside from cases of denial of justice.[205] Situations of this kind have included disrespect of due process and procedural propriety, arbitrariness, and obstruction of the investment through abusive proceedings.[206] In *Deutsche Bank v. Sri Lanka*, for instance, the ICSID tribunal found that a Supreme Court decision constituted a breach of FET as it was contrary to due process and "issued for political reasons".[207] **165**

Protection against unlawful expropriation has also sometimes been found to cover misconduct by domestic courts. Although, as noted in *Tatneft v. Ukraine*, the prohibition of unlawful expropriation is mainly concerned with the protection of property rights against the government abusing its legislative or executive power and is thus mostly related to administrative and legislative acts, "the issue of whether in addition an act of expropriation can also originate in the judiciary [is] not in principle **166**

[201] See Demirkol (2018), p. 28.

[202] See, e.g., CETA, Article 8, para. 10(2), providing that "[a] Party breaches the obligation of fair and equitable treatment referenced in paragraph 1 if a measure or series of measures constitutes: (a) denial of justice in criminal, civil or administrative proceedings; (b) fundamental breach of due process, including a fundamental breach of transparency, in judicial and administrative proceedings; (c) manifest arbitrariness; (d) targeted discrimination on manifestly wrongful grounds, such as gender, race or religious belief; (e) abusive treatment of investors, such as coercion, duress and harassment [. . .]".

[203] *Saipem S.p.A. v. The People's Republic of Bangladesh*, ICSID Case No. ARB/05/07, Award, 30 June 2009, para 181.

[204] See *Chevron Corporation (USA) and Texaco Petroleum Company (USA) v. The Republic of Ecuador*, UNCITRAL, PCA Case No. 34877, Partial Award on the Merits, 30 March 2010, para. 322; Demirkol (2018), p. 29.

[205] See generally Demirkol (2018), pp. 34–39.

[206] *Ibid.*

[207] See *Deutsche Bank AG v. Democratic Socialist Republic of Sri Lanka*, ICSID Case No. ARB/09/2, Award, 31 October 2012, paras. 478–480.

excluded under interactional law and BIT protection".[208] The tribunal in *Eli Lilly v. Canada* also noted that "[a]s a matter of broad proposition, [...] it is possible to contemplate circumstances in which a judicial act (or omission) may engage questions of expropriation under NAFTA Article 1110, such as, perhaps, in circumstances in which a judicial decision crystallizes a taking alleged to be contrary to NAFTA Article 1110".[209] In *Middle East Cement v. Egypt*, the tribunal found that "though normally, a seizure and auction ordered by the national courts does not qualify as a taking, they can be a 'measure the effects of which would be tantamount to expropriation' if they are not taken 'under due process of law'".[210] The tribunal in *Garanti Koza v. Turkmenistan Award* held that "a seizure of property by a court as the result of normal domestic legal process does not amount to an expropriation under international law unless there was an element of serious and fundamental impropriety about the legal process".[211]

167 A few tribunals have also examined whether the "full protection and security" standard could encompass protection from domestic courts' misconduct. In *Frontier Petroleum v. Czech Republic*, the tribunal held that in respect of the acts of the judiciary "full protection and security" means that the State is under an obligation to make a functioning system of courts and legal remedies available to the investor. It observed, however, that "not every failure to obtain redress is a violation of the principle of full protection and security" and "[e]ven a decision that in the eyes of an outside observer, such as an international tribunal, is 'wrong' would not automatically lead to State responsibility as long as the courts have acted in good faith and have reached decisions that are reasonably tenable".[212]

168 Finally, a few IIAs contain a so-called "effective means standard" clause. As noted by the *Chevron v. Ecuador I* tribunal, provisions of this type are relatively rare.[213] One such example is Article 10, para. 12, of the ECT, to which Switzerland is a party, which provides as follows:

---

[208]See *OAO Tatneft v. Ukraine*, UNCITRAL PCA Case No. 2008-8, Award on the Merits, 29 July 2014, paras. 459–461.

[209]*Eli Lilly and Company v. The Government of Canada*, UNCITRAL, ICSID Case No. UNCT/14/2, Award, 16 March 2017, para. 221.

[210]*Middle East Cement Shipping and Handling Co. S.A. v. Arab Republic of Egypt*, ICSID Case No. ARB/99/6, Award, 12 April 2002, para. 139.

[211]See *Garanti Koza LLP v. Turkmenistan*, ICSID Case No. ARB/11/20, Award, 19 December 2016, para. 365.

[212]See *Frontier Petroleum Services Ltd. v. The Czech Republic*, Final Award, 12 November 2010, para. 273.

[213]*Chevron Corporation (USA) and Texaco Petroleum Company (USA) v. The Republic of Ecuador*, UNCITRAL, PCA Case No. 34877, Partial Award on the Merits, 30 March 2010, paras. 241–244, finding also that the effective means provision in the U.S.-Ecuador BIT constitutes a *lex specialis* and not a mere restatement of the law on denial of justice, which entails that a distinct and potentially less-demanding test is applicable under the effective means standard as compared to denial of justice under customary international law.

> Each Contracting Party shall ensure that its domestic law provides effective means for the assertion of claims and the enforcement of rights with respect to Investments, investment agreements, and investment authorisations.

According to the *Amto v. Ukraine* tribunal, the "fundamental criterion" of an "effective means" for the assertion of claims and the enforcement of rights within the meaning of Article 10, para. 12, of the ECT, is "law and the rule of law"; "[t]here must be legislation for the recognition and enforcement of property and contractual rights"; "[a]n effective means of the assertion of claims and the enforcement of rights also requires secondary rules of procedure so that the principles and objectives of the legislation can be translated by the investor into effective action in the domestic tribunals".[214] The effective means standard was further discussed in the *White Industries v. India* award, which is addressed *infra*. 169

3.4.3 Domestic Court Decisions on Commercial Arbitration

One particular area in which investment arbitration has been used as a forum for the adjudication of disputes arising out of domestic courts' alleged misconduct concerns national court decisions about the enforcement of arbitration agreements and the annulment or enforcement of arbitral awards in commercial matters under the NYC.[215] In these instances, investment tribunals have exercised a sort of "super-supervisory" role over domestic courts' conduct relating to commercial arbitration.[216] These cases further highlight the complex interaction between various dispute resolution mechanisms that may have a bearing on a private party's investment and involve commercial arbitration, domestic courts, and investment arbitration. 170

As an illustration, in the dispute between Frontier Petroleum and the Czech Republic mentioned earlier, the investment tribunal assessed whether a national court's refusal to enforce an arbitral award under the NYC for reasons of incompatibility with international public policy breached the applicable IIA. The tribunal dismissed the respondent's argument that an investment arbitration tribunal lacks power to review a national court's decision rendered under the NYC. It considered that its role was "to determine whether the refusal of the Czech courts to recognize and enforce the Final Award in full violate[d] Article III(1) of the BIT, i.e., the fair and equitable treatment standard".[217] It went on to say that "in order to answer this question the tribunal must ask whether the Czech courts' refusal amounts to an abuse 171

[214] *Limited Liability Company Amto v. Ukraine*, SCC Case No. 080/2005, Final Award, 26 March 2008, p. 52.

[215] See generally Kaufmann-Kohler (2013), pp. 153–174.

[216] Kaufmann-Kohler (2013), p. 154.

[217] *Frontier Petroleum Services Ltd. v. The Czech Republic*, Final Award, 12 November 2010, para. 525.

of rights contrary to the international principle of good faith".[218] Recognizing that "States enjoy a certain margin of appreciation in determining what their own conception of international public policy is",[219] the question, in the tribunal's view, was whether "the decision by the Czech courts [was] *reasonably tenable* and made in *good faith*".[220]

172 *Saipem v. Bangladesh* involved the conduct of domestic courts relating to an ICC arbitration seated in the respondent's capital, Dhaka.[221] During the ICC arbitration, the Bangladeshi courts intervened in several ways, including issuing an injunction restraining Saipem from continuing with the ICC arbitration and revoking the authority of the ICC tribunal. Once the ICC tribunal had nevertheless rendered its award, the courts ruled that, because of the revocation of authority, there "was no award in the eye of the law" which could either be set aside or enforced.[222] Saipem then initiated ICSID proceedings under the Italy-Bangladesh BIT. The ICSID tribunal held that the Bangladeshi courts had taken measures amounting to unlawful expropriation.[223] The measures also constituted an abuse of rights under international law[224] and breached the NYC.[225]

173 The UNCITRAL award in *White Industries v. India* provides a further example of an investment tribunal's review of a decision of national courts relating to a commercial arbitration award.[226] The investor initially sought enforcement of an ICC award in India. After 9 years of complex litigation involving enforcement and setting aside proceedings (none of which resulted in a determination), White Industries initiated an investment arbitration invoking the Australia-India BIT.[227] The

---

[218] *Frontier Petroleum Services Ltd. v. The Czech Republic*, Final Award, 12 November 2010, para. 525.

[219] *Frontier Petroleum Services Ltd. v. The Czech Republic*, Final Award, 12 November 2010, para. 527.

[220] *Frontier Petroleum Services Ltd. v. The Czech Republic*, Final Award, 12 November 2010, para. 527 (emphasis in the original).

[221] *Saipem S.p.A. v. The People's Republic of Bangladesh*, ICSID Case No. ARB/05/07, Decision on Jurisdiction and Recommendation on Provisional Measures, 21 March 2007 and Award, 30 June 2009. For commentaries on *Saipem*, see Radicati di Brozolo and Malintoppi (2010), pp. 993–1012; Mourre and Vagenheim (2010), pp. 843–866.

[222] *Saipem S.p.A. v. The People's Republic of Bangladesh*, ICSID Case No. ARB/05/07, Decision on Jurisdiction and Recommendation on Provisional Measures, 21 March 2007, paras. 26–36.

[223] *Saipem S.p.A. v. The People's Republic of Bangladesh*, ICSID Case No. ARB/05/07, Award, 30 June 2009, paras. 129, 133, 201–202.

[224] *Saipem S.p.A. v. The People's Republic of Bangladesh*, ICSID Case No. ARB/05/07, Award, 30 June 2009, paras. 160–161.

[225] *Saipem S.p.A. v. The People's Republic of Bangladesh*, ICSID Case No. ARB/05/07, Award, 30 June 2009, paras. 167–168, 170.

[226] *White Industries Australia Limited v. The Republic of India*, UNCITRAL, Final Award, 30 November 2011.

[227] *White Industries Australia Limited v. The Republic of India*, UNCITRAL, Final Award, 30 November 2011, paras. 3.2.1–3.2.65.

investment treaty tribunal dismissed the claims of expropriation,[228] FET[229] and denial of justice.[230] However, it found that the duration of the enforcement proceedings (which included more than 5 years on the docket of the Supreme Court) amounted to a breach of India's obligation to provide "effective means of asserting claims and enforcing rights".[231]

In sum, these and other cases[232] involving review by investment tribunals of national court decisions in relation to commercial arbitration matters show that States, through their courts, enjoy a level of discretion in the application and interpretation of the applicable legal framework, which is most often the NYC. Most mistakes made in this exercise of application and interpretation of the law will trigger no international responsibility. It is only when the national court's mistake reaches the high threshold of an egregious misconduct that redress may be sought from an international dispute resolution body.[233] **174**

References

Allen BE, Soave T (2014) Jurisdictional overlap in WTO dispute settlement and investment arbitration. Arbitr Int 30(1):1–58

Bernardini P (2010) ICSID versus non-ICSID investment treaty arbitration. In: Fernández-Ballesteros MA, Lozano DA (eds) Liber Amicorum Bernardo Cremades. Wolters Kluwer, Alphen aan den Rijn, pp 159–188

Besson S (2016) Droit international public, 3rd edn. Stämpfli Verlag AG, Bern, pp 333–337

Bjorklund AK (2004) Waiver and the exhaustion of local remedies rule in NAFTA jurisprudence. In: Weiler T (ed) NAFTA investment law and arbitration: past issues, current practice, future prospects. Brill|Nijhoff, Leiden, pp 253–286

Bonnitcha J, Skovgaard Poulsen LN, Waibel M (2017) The political economy of the investment treaty regime. Oxford University Press, Oxford, pp 84–85

Brauch MD (2017) Exhaustion of local remedies in international investment law, Best Practices Series. International Institute for Sustainable Development, Winnipeg, pp 7–12

Bronckers M (2015) Is Investor-State Dispute Settlement (ISDS) superior to litigation before domestic courts?An EU view on bilateral trade agreements. J Int Econ law 18:655–677

Brower CN, Goodman REM (1991) Provisional measures and the protection of ICSID jurisdictional exclusivity against municipal proceedings. ICSID Rev Foreign Invest Law J 6 (2):431–461

[228] *White Industries Australia Limited v. The Republic of India*, UNCITRAL, Final Award, 30 November 2011, Section 12.

[229] *White Industries Australia Limited v. The Republic of India*, UNCITRAL, Final Award, 30 November 2011, paras. 10.1–10.3.

[230] *White Industries Australia Limited v. The Republic of India*, UNCITRAL, Final Award, 30 November 2011, Section 10.4.

[231] See in particular *White Industries Australia Limited v. The Republic of India*, UNCITRAL, Final Award, 30 November 2011, Section 11.

[232] See, e.g. *ATA Construction, Industrial and Trading Company v. The Hashemite Kingdom of Jordan*, ICSID Case No. ARB/08/2, Award, 18 May 2010.

[233] See Radicati di Brozolo and Malintoppi (2010), pp. 993–1012.

Collins L (1992-III) Provisional and protective measures in international litigation. In: Recueil des Cours 218, vol 234. Martinus Nijhoff, Leiden, p 99

Crawford J (2008) Treaty and contract in investment arbitration. Arbitr Int 24(3):351–374

Crawford J, Grant TD (2007) Local remedies, exhaustion of. In: Wolfrum R (ed) Max Planck Encyclopedia of Public International Law. Oxford University Press, Oxford

De Luca A (2016) Direct Effect of EU's Investment Agreements and the Energy Charter Treaty in the EU, Rivista Eurojus.it, 15 November 2016, Available at http://rivista.eurojus.it/direct-effect-of-eus-investment-agreements-and-the-energy-charter-treaty-in-the-eu/

Delaume GR (1983) ICSID arbitration and the courts. Am J Int Law 77(4):784–803

Delaume GR (1984) ICSID arbitration in practice. Int Tax Bus Lawyer 2:58–78

Demirkol B (2018) Judicial acts and investment treaty arbitration. Cambridge University Press, Cambridge

Dodge WS (2006) Investor-state dispute settlement between developed countries: reflections on the Australia-United states free trade agreement. Vanderbilt J Transnational Law 39(1):1–37

Dolzer R, Schreuer CH (2012) Principles of international investment law, 2nd edn. Oxford University Press, Oxford, p 235

Douglas Z (2004) The hybrid foundations of investment treaty arbitration. Br Yearb Int Law 74 (1):151–289

Douglas Z (2012) The international law of investment claims. Cambridge University Press, Cambridge, pp 98–99

Douglas Z (2014) International responsibility for domestic adjudication: denial of justice deconstructed. Int Comp Law Q 63(4):867–900

Fix-Fierro H, López-Ayllón S (1997) The impact of globalization on the reform of the state and the law in Latin America. Houston J Int Law 19(3):785–801

Friedland PD (1986) Provisional measures and ICSID arbitration. Arbitr Int 2(4):335–357

García-Castrillón CO (2016) Spain and investment arbitration: the renewable energy explosion, investor-state arbitration series, Paper No. 17, November 2016. Centre for International Governance Innovation, Waterloo

David Gaukrodger (2018) Appointing authorities and the selection of arbitrators in investor-state dispute settlement: an overview, OECD Consultation Paper, March 2018, paras. 205–222, Available at http://www.oecd.org/investment/investment-policy/ISDS-Appointing-Authorities-Arbitration-March-2018.pdf

Gil R (2009) ICSID provisional measures to enjoin parallel domestic litigation. World Arbitr Mediation Rev 3(4–5):353–602

Ginsburg T (2005) International substitutes for domestic institutions: bilateral investment treaties and governance. Int Rev Law Econ 25(1):107–123

Giroud S (2012) Enforcement against state assets and execution of ICSID awards in Switzerland: how Swiss courts deal with immunity defences. ASA Bull 30(4):758–766

Hanessian G, Duggal K (2017) The final 2015 Indian Model BIT: is this the change the world wishes to see? ICSID Rev Foreign Invest Law J 32(1):216–226

Hathaway OA, McElroy S, Solow SA (2012) International law at home: enforcing treaties in U.S. Courts. Yale J Int Law 37(1):51–106

Hepburn J (2009) India agrees new investment treaty text with Colombia, Belarus And Taiwan, advancing some of its key concerns such as partial exhaustion and human rights [Updated], IAReporter, (1 January 2019)

Hober K, Eliasson N (2018) Review of non-ICSID awards by National Courts. In: Yannaca-Small K (ed) Arbitration under international investment agreements, a guide to the key issues, 2nd edn. Oxford University Press, Oxford, pp 759–796

Johnson L (2015) Aligning Swiss investment treaties with sustainable development: an assessment of current policy coherence and options for future action. Columbia Centre on Sustainable Investment, New York, p 14

Kaiser K (2013) Treaties, direct applicability. In: Wolfrum R (ed) Max Planck encyclopedia of public international law, 2nd edn. Oxford University Press, Oxford

Kalderimis D (2016) The authority of investment treaty tribunals to issue orders restraining domestic court proceedings. ICSID Rev Foreign Invest Law J 31(3):549–575

Kaufmann-Kohler G (2013) Commercial arbitration before international courts and tribunals – reviewing abusive conduct of domestic courts. Arbitr Int 29(2):153–174

Kaufmann-Kohler G, Rigozzi A (2015) International arbitration law and practice in Switzerland. Oxford University Press, Oxford, p 57

Kaufmann-Kohler G, Antonietti A, Potestà M (2018) Interim relief in investment arbitration. In: Yannaca-Small K (ed) Arbitration under international investment agreements, a guide to the key issues, 2nd edn. Oxford University Press, Oxford, pp 647–649

Kjos HE (2016) International law through the National Prism: the role of domestic law and jurisprudence in shaping international investment law. In: Reinisch A, Footer ME, Binder C (eds) International law and ...: Select proceedings of the European Society of International Law. Hart Publishing, Oxford, p 84

Kriebaum U (2009) Local remedies and the standards for the protection of foreign investment. In: Binder C, Kriebaum U, Reinisch A, Wittich S (eds) International investment law for the 21st century. Oxford University Press, Oxford, pp 417–462

Mourre A, Vagenheim A (2010) Some comments on denial of justice in public and private international law after Loewen and Saipem. In: Fernández-Ballesteros MA, Lozano DA (eds) Liber Amicorum Bernardo Cremades. Wolters Kluwer, Alphen aan den Rijn, pp 843–866

Muchlinski P (2009) Diplomatic protection of foreign investments. In: Binder C, Kriebaum U, Reinisch A, Wittich S (eds) International investment law for the 21st century. Oxford university Press, Oxford, p 345

Ortiz AL, Ugalde-Revilla P, Chinn C (2016) The role of national courts in ICSID arbitration. In: Baltag C (ed) ICSID Convention after 50 years: unsettled issues. Wolters Kluwer, Alphen aan den Rijn, pp 329–362

Parra AR (1993) The practices and experience of ICSID in ICC, Conservatory and Provisional Measures in International Arbitration, ICC Publication No. 519, pp 37–44

Paulsson J (2005) Denial of justice in international law. Cambridge University Press, Cambridge

Pohl J, Mashigo K, Nohen A (2012) Dispute settlement provisions in international investment agreements: a large sample survey, OECD working papers on international investment, 2012/02. OECD Publishing, Paris, p 14

Porterfield M (2015) Exhaustion of local remedies in investor-state dispute settlement: an idea whose time has come? Yale J Int Law 41:1–12

Puig S (2013) Investor-state tribunals and constitutional courts: the Mexican Sweeteners Saga. Mexican Law Rev 5(2):199–243

Radicati di Brozolo L, Malintoppi L (2010) Unlawful interference with international arbitration by national courts of the seat in the aftermath of Saipem v. Bangladesh. In: Fernández-Ballesteros MA, Lozano DA (eds) Liber Amicorum Bernardo Cremades. Wolters Kluwer, Alphen aan den Rijn, pp 993–1012

Radjai N, Stirnimann FX (2013) Investment arbitration. In: Arroyo M (ed) Arbitration in Switzerland – the practitioner's guide: commentary. Wolters Kluwer, Alphen aan den Rijn, pp 1049–1112

Ranjan P, Anand P (2017) The 2016 model Indian bilateral investment treaty: a critical deconstruction. Northwest J Int Law Bus 38(1):1–55

Reinisch A (2018) Enforcement of investment treaty awards. In: Yannaca-Small K (ed) Arbitration under international investment agreements, a guide to the key issues, 2nd edn. Oxford University Press, Oxford, pp 797–822

Scherer M, Heiskanen V, Moss S (2009) Domestic review of investment treaty arbitration: the Swiss experience. ASA Bull 27(2):256–279

Schreuer CH (2004) Travelling the BIT route: of waiting periods, umbrella clauses and forks in the road. J World Invest Trade 5(2):231–256

Schreuer CH (2005) Calvo's grandchild: the return of local remedies in investment arbitration. Law Pract Int Courts Tribunals 4(1):1–17

Schreuer CH (2010) Interaction of international tribunals and domestic courts in investment law. In: Contemporary issues in international arbitration and mediation: the fordham papers, vol 4. Brill Nijhoff, Leiden, pp 71–94

Schreuer CH, Malintoppi L, Reinisch A, Sinclair A (2009) The ICSID Convention—a commentary, 2nd edn. Cambridge University Press, Cambridge

Shany Y (2007) Regulating jurisdictional relations between national and international courts. Oxford University Press, Oxford

Sornarajah M (2010) The international law on foreign investment. Cambridge University Press, Cambridge, p 221

Spiermann O (2009) Premature treaty claims. In: Binder C, Kriebaum U, Reinisch A, Wittich S (eds) International investment law for the 21st century. Oxford University Press, Oxford, pp 463–489

Tietje C, Baetens F (2014) The Impact of Investor-State-Dispute Settlement (ISDS) in the transatlantic trade and investment partnership, Study prepared for the Minister for Foreign Trade and Development Cooperation and the Ministry of Foreign Affairs of the Netherlands, p 95

Wegen G, Markert L (2010) Food for thought on fork-in-the-road — a clause awakens from its hibernation. In: Zeiler G, Welser I et al (eds) Austrian yearbook on international arbitration, vol 2010, pp 269–292

Chapter 4
The Path to Reform of ISDS: What Role for National Courts?

4.1 Introduction

Chapter 3 has reviewed the areas of interaction between investment arbitration tribunals and national courts in the *current* framework. This Chap. 4 examines how the role of national courts may change under each of the main scenarios for reform of the investor-State dispute settlement system that States are presently considering. The design options and legal challenges associated with these reform proposals have been analyzed elsewhere,[1] as has the potential of each of them to address the alleged concerns with the existing system.[2] With a view to taking that analysis further, this chapter seeks to outline what (if any) role domestic courts may play within each of the reform proposals. **175.**

To that end, we will consider four reform scenarios which envisage maintaining or establishing a mechanism for the resolution of disputes concerning an investment *on the international plane*, namely: **176.**

a. Improvement of the current investor-State arbitration system ("investment arbitration improved") (*infra* at Sect. 4.2);
b. Addition of an AM to the current investment arbitration regime (*infra* at Sect. 4.3);
c. Introduction of a MIC (with or without a built-in appeal) (*infra* at Sect. 4.4); and
d. Replacement of the current system with SSDS (*infra* at Sect. 4.5).

[1]See Gabrielle Kaufmann-Kohler and Michele Potestà (2016), *First CIDS Report*; Gabrielle Kaufmann-Kohler and Michele Potestà (2017), *CIDS Supplemental Report*.

[2]See the "concept papers" prepared by members of the Academic Forum on ISDS on "Matching Concerns and Reform Options", available at https://www.cids.ch/academic-forum-concept-papers.

G. Kaufmann-Kohler, M. Potestà, *Investor-State Dispute Settlement and National Courts*, European Yearbook of International Economic Law,
https://doi.org/10.1007/978-3-030-44164-7_4

The options just mentioned are the main ones advanced in the discussions around reform of the investor-State dispute settlement system[3] and reflect the principal alternatives available for the design of dispute settlement systems. They also represent the broad spectrum of positions and views expressed in recent State practice and in the debate surrounding investment arbitration.

177. Reforming investor-State dispute settlement with an eye to considering the appropriate role that domestic courts may or should play within these different reform scenarios requires examining primarily the models of jurisdictional coordination between national and international fora and the role of national courts in support and control of these international fora (if any). The current framework of interaction between national and international tribunals, discussed *supra* at Sects. 3.2 and 3.3, may thus serve as a useful starting point to delineate relations between national and international tribunals for the reform efforts. In the following analysis, however, it will be seen that many of the existing rules examined earlier in this study would require adaptation to the new institutional settings envisaged by some of the reform options.[4] Beyond those already examined, two other "jurisdiction-regulating" models (to use Yuval Shany's terminology)[5] and their potential applicability to the investment framework will be reviewed, i.e. (i) preliminary rulings from domestic courts to international tribunals; and (ii) complementarity between domestic and international courts (*infra* at Sect. 4.6).

178. In addition to the four reform options enumerated in para. 176 above which entail an international remedy (whether investor-State or State-to-State), a fifth possible reform outcome is sometimes advocated by certain stakeholders, i.e. the replacement of the current system with domestic courts only, for all or some categories of disputes concerning investments. This fifth reform scenario will also be considered (*infra* at Sect. 4.7).

179. Before delving into each of these reform options, two observations are in order. First, in terms of system design, not only can international mechanisms be combined with national courts in various ways (which is the subject of this chapter), international mechanisms may also be combined with other international mechanisms. For instance, States could design dispute settlement mechanisms in which investment arbitration is combined with SSDS for certain questions of interpretation of the IIA.[6] This latter type of combination is not systematically examined as it falls outside the scope of this study. Second, the five reform scenarios that have been chosen for discussion in this chapter are limited to dispute settlement mechanisms that lead to a *binding* decision. This means that this study does not examine methods such as

---

[3]See UNCITRAL Working Group III, *Possible reform of investor-State dispute settlement (ISDS) - Note by the Secretariat*, A/CN.9/WG.III/WP.166. See also generally Roberts (2018), pp. 410–432.

[4]The following sections, by contrast, do not address State conduct for liability of domestic courts (discussed *supra* in chapter 3.4) which is a substantive question and thus outside the scope of the current reform discussions which are focused exclusively on dispute settlement and procedure.

[5]See generally Shany (2007), pp. 27–77.

[6]See Potestà (2015), pp. 249–273.

mediation, conciliation, ombudsman, etc. This limitation in no way implies any judgment on the usefulness of these alternative mechanisms, which may well deserve to be the subject of a further study. It should also be noted that in any event non-binding methods of dispute resolution are usually combined with one of the binding options discussed here.

Finally, in terms of instruments for effecting the changes that are discussed in the following sections, depending on the reform option chosen these may involve (i) the amendment of IIAs; (ii) the negotiation of an opt-in Mauritius Convention-type plurilateral treaty able to effect changes *en bloc* for a number of treaties; and/or (iii) the negotiation of statutes or constitutive treaties for the establishment of new international bodies (the AM Statute or MIC Statute).[7] **180.**

4.2 Investment Arbitration "Improved"

One option that is currently being considered is the reform of investment arbitration through "incremental" changes or improvements, i.e. reform short of creating new standing bodies. "Improving" investment arbitration in this manner may for instance include effecting changes in respect of the appointment of and rules of conduct for arbitrators. This may include providing for appointment predominantly by arbitral institutions or effected jointly by disputing parties, creating a roster-system, adopting ethical rules, reinforcing procedures for the dismissal of frivolous claims, enhancing transparency of proceedings and the like. These more "limited" changes will in and of themselves not affect the relationship between the "improved" investor-State arbitral mechanism and the domestic courts. Thus, the various modes of interaction between national courts and international tribunals described *supra* in Chap. 3 would continue to apply. **181.**

The panoply of solutions on the coordination between investment tribunals and domestic courts described previously can, however, guide States wishing to recalibrate the coordination of investment arbitration and domestic courts in a different way from what they have done so far, in line with their policy preferences.[8] States may for instance introduce, remove, or re-modulate exhaustion of local remedies requirements, domestic litigation requirements, fork-in-the-road clauses or waiver clauses in their existing and future IIAs. As mentioned previously, certain more recent treaties already formulate fork-in-the-road and waiver clauses with a **182.**

---

[7]See generally on these questions, Gabrielle Kaufmann-Kohler and Michele Potestà (2016), *First CIDS Report*, Section VII.

[8]For suggestions on the more meaningful role that exhaustion of local remedies could play, see for instance the following submissions made by States in the UNCITRAL WGIII discussions: A/CN.9/WG.III/WP.156, Submission from the Government of Indonesia, para. 17; A/CN.9/WG.III/WP.161, Submission from the Government of Morocco, Annex I, paras. 9 and 14; A/CN.9/WG.III/WP.176, Submission from the Government of South Africa, paras. 43–46.

view to remedying certain shortcomings arising from what have been viewed as excessively formalistic applications of the so-called triple identity test.[9]

4.3 Investment Arbitration + Appeal

183. This reform option envisages the creation of an AM for awards rendered in investor-State arbitration proceedings.[10] The creation of an appeal layer does not in and of itself have an effect on the relationship between the first-instance arbitral jurisdiction and domestic courts, which absent specific rules would continue to be governed by the framework provided under the specific IIA. Thus, for instance, if an IIA provides for an 18-month domestic litigation requirement as a pre-condition to accessing the arbitral tribunal, the addition of an appeal will in and of itself not affect such requirement which will continue to exist as far as the first level of jurisdiction is concerned.

184. Nevertheless, the introduction of an AM may significantly affect the role of domestic courts in controlling the arbitration, especially at the annulment and enforcement stages. These aspects will need to be carefully examined if and when an appellate mechanism for investor-State arbitral awards is established. The legal issues to be considered in this context are significant and require taking into account the distinctions between ICSID and non-ICSID arbitrations, which are subject to different legal regimes.[11] This holds especially true if States were to establish one, single, stand-alone AM with appellate jurisdiction over both ICSID and non-ICSID awards.[12] The following discussion assumes (i) the creation of such a stand-alone AM (as opposed to multiple treaty-specific AMs), and (ii), as far as ICSID awards are concerned, the permissibility of an *inter se* modification of the ICSID Convention pursuant to Article 41 of the VCLT, on which these authors have taken an affirmative view.[13]

185. In designing an AM for investor-State arbitral awards, one threshold question requiring consideration is whether the new AM should be subject to a national *lex*

---

[9]See *supra* para. 83.

[10]See generally Gabrielle Kaufmann-Kohler and Michele Potestà (2016), *First CIDS Report*, section VI.

[11]See *supra* paras. 118–119.

[12]The ICSID Secretariat 2004 paper, for instance, suggested that the creation of an ICSID Appeals Facility could apply to ICSID and non-ICSID awards. See ICSID Secretariat, Discussion Paper 2004, Annex, para. 1 (suggesting that the ICSID Appeals Facility "would best be designed for use in conjunction with both forms of ICSID arbitration, UNCITRAL Rules arbitration and any other form of arbitration provided for in the investor-to-State dispute-settlement provisions of investment treaties").

[13]See Gabrielle Kaufmann-Kohler and Michele Potestà (2016), *First CIDS Report*, Section VII.B.2. See also McGarry and Ostřanský (2017), pp. 1001–1013. For a different view, see Jansen Calamita (2017), pp. 585–627.

arbitri (like non-ICSID investment arbitrations) or be de-localized and governed only by international law (like ICSID arbitrations).[14] One possibility would be that the procedural law applicable to the AM proceedings would be the same as the procedural law governing the first-instance proceedings. Thus, to give an example, proceedings in an UNCITRAL investment arbitration seated in Switzerland would be subject to Chapter 12 of the PILA for both the first instance and appeal proceedings[15]; whereas in an ICSID arbitration subject to appeal, both the first instance and appeal proceedings would be governed by international law. This "dual track" would entail two types of legal regimes applicable to appeal proceedings, including for awards rendered under the same IIA, if the IIA provides for a choice between ICSID and non-ICSID arbitration. A different possibility to be explored would be to have a completely de-localized AM procedure subject only to international law for all types of appeal awards. The legal consequences of these choices are important because, as seen above in Sect. 3.3, national courts potentially play a different role in an arbitration governed by a national *lex arbitri* as opposed to an "a-national" arbitration.

The treaty establishing the AM (the AM Statute) should thus regulate these matters to avoid uncertainties, in particular as far as annulment and enforcement are concerned, which are the two areas in which court intervention will be most relevant. **186.**

Starting with the relationship between a potential AM and annulment, these authors have taken the view that the prospective AM should *substitute* rather than be combined with any annulment-type review present under national law or the ICSID Convention.[16] In other words, appeal and annulment remedies appear mutually exclusive. This is in part because grounds for appeal are normally broader than (and thus already include) the usual grounds for annulment.[17] Furthermore, providing for the possibility of annulment of appeal awards would *de facto* create a three-tier dispute settlement system, which would go against the objective of efficiency in terms of time and costs.[18] **187.**

With this assumption in mind (i.e. that no annulment remedies will be provided for appeal awards), for non-ICSID arbitrations, the AM Statute should exclude any role of domestic courts for the purposes of annulment of appeal awards, i.e. the AM Statute should provide for a waiver of judicial review in respect of awards rendered by the AM, in order to avoid a duplication of remedies.[19] Because not all domestic laws would necessarily recognize such a waiver as a valid agreement to exclude the **188.**

[14] See Gabrielle Kaufmann-Kohler and Michele Potestà (2016), *First CIDS Report*, paras. 193–195.

[15] For this solution in the field of commercial arbitration see, e.g., AAA Optional Appellate Arbitration Rules, Rule A-14 ("Unless all parties and the appeal tribunal agree otherwise, the appeal shall be conducted at the same place of arbitration as the underlying arbitration").

[16] See Gabrielle Kaufmann-Kohler and Michele Potestà (2016), *First CIDS Report*, paras. 115, 196.

[17] *Ibid.*

[18] *Ibid.* On this point, see also the discussion in van den Berg (2019), pp. 104–107.

[19] See Gabrielle Kaufmann-Kohler and Michele Potestà (2016), *First CIDS Report*, para. 197.

right to seek annulment before their courts, Contracting Parties should consider passing legislation to this effect. In that context, it should also be provided that the arbitration (including the appeals phase, should it not be de-localized for all types of proceedings) must be seated in a State that is a party to the AM Statute. Otherwise, in circumstances where the seat is situated in a third State, there is a risk that such State would not recognize the waiver of judicial review as valid. With regard to ICSID awards, the AM Statute should similarly exclude any annulment of ICSID awards under Article 52 of the ICSID Convention.

189. With regard to enforcement, the question arises as to the effects of adding an AM layer on the enforcement of an award which has been subject to appeal under the AM.[20] As a preliminary remark, it is important to note that, as is the case with annulment, any specific enforcement regime set out in the AM Statute will only bind the Contracting Parties to the Statute.[21]

190. With regard to enforcement in their territories, Contracting Parties may opt for one single enforcement regime for all appeal awards (whether rendered in non-ICSID or ICSID arbitrations). Alternatively, they could put in place distinct enforcement regimes depending on whether the first-instance award is an ICSID or a non-ICSID award. The former could for instance be enforced pursuant to an Article 54-type rule, whereas the latter would be subject to the NYC regime. It should be noted that if States opt for a dual enforcement regime, depending on the nature of the underlying arbitration, there could potentially be two different enforcement regimes applicable to appeal awards rendered under the same IIA, where the IIA provides for an option between ICSID and non-ICSID arbitrations. This, in practice, would mean that the scope of review of domestic courts at enforcement would be broader for certain awards (Article V of the NYC) than for others (ICSID Convention Article 54-type provision).

191. With regard to enforcement in third States, an award subject to an appeal or the appeal award itself[22] would be enforceable under the NYC,[23] because the addition of an appellate layer does not change the nature of the arbitration process.[24] This is true, of course, for a non-ICSID award that is subject to appeal. With regard to ICSID

---

[20]On enforcement of appeal awards see Gabrielle Kaufmann-Kohler and Michele Potestà (2016), *First CIDS Report*, Section V.E; van den Berg (2019), pp. 85–104.

[21]VCLT, Article 34.

[22]Under the NYC, the first-instance award can be refused recognition and enforcement if it is being appealed or is still open to appeal, under Article V, para. 1(e) ("award that has not yet become binding"). For the position in Switzerland, see Kaufmann-Kohler and Rigozzi (2015), p. 528. As noted by van den Berg, "[t]he IIA can set forth whether a first instance award can be enforced pending arbitral appeal or the period of time for lodging the appeal. If no such provisions are contained in the IIA (or rules of procedure issued thereunder), the fallback interpretation can be relied upon, i.e. the award becomes binding at the moment when it is no longer open to an appeal." (see van den Berg 2019, para. 141).

[23]Gabrielle Kaufmann-Kohler and Michele Potestà (2016), *First CIDS Report*, para. 199.

[24]Gabrielle Kaufmann-Kohler and Michele Potestà (2016), *First CIDS Report*, Sections VI.E and V.E.2.c.

awards subject to an appeal, non-parties to the *inter se* modification would not be bound by the special enforcement regime that were to be established along the lines of Article 54 of the ICSID Convention. Rather, they would be in a situation similar to that of non-ICSID Contracting Parties in respect of an ICSID award. In other words, they would have to enforce the ICSID award in accordance with the NYC.[25] This matter can also be viewed from a different angle. Suppose the AM Statute were to provide a waiver of the grounds for refusal of enforcement (which provision would bind both the State Contracting Parties and the investor which accepts to arbitrate under the treaty). What effect would such a waiver have on third States? It would seem that it would be for each (third) State to determine to what extent a waiver of the grounds for refusal of enforcement included in the AM Statute would be valid in their own legal system. That being so, it is doubtful that the waiver would be effective. Even if specific language is used, as is required under some legislation, it would remain that "the grounds for refusal of enforcement in paragraph 2 of Article V of the New York Convention are legally not capable of being waived or contracted out of".[26]

In sum, with regard to the role of domestic courts in a reform scenario providing an AM for investor-State arbitral awards, the domestic courts' role at annulment is susceptible to being significantly curtailed when compared with their role under the existing regime vis-à-vis non-ICSID arbitrations. This is a natural consequence of the addition of a second layer of review which makes the courts' supervisory role largely unnecessary. In enforcement matters, domestic courts are likely to keep a role in third countries not parties to the AM Statute, as well as in Contracting Parties depending on the enforcement regime set out in the Statute. **192.**

4.4 Multilateral Investment Court

If a MIC is created, how is the role of domestic court going to change?[27] Once again, based on the categories of jurisdictional coordination reviewed in chapter 3.2 above, States may envisage designing a role for domestic courts in the sequential or alternative modes previously examined. As an example of a regulation of the interplay between domestic courts and a standing investment court, one can look to the constitutive instrument of the Arab Investment Court, which provides for a fork-in-the-road clause.[28] **193.**

[25]See Gabrielle Kaufmann-Kohler and Michele Potestà (2016), *First CIDS Report*, paras. 200, 245.

[26]van den Berg (2019), para. 149.

[27]The following discussion assumes that the prospective MIC will be regulated by a new "MIC Statute" and "Rules of the Court", rather than by modified arbitration rules.

[28]See Unified Agreement for the Investment of Arab Capital in the Arab States (opened for signature 26 November 1980, entered into force 7 September 1981), Articles 31 and 32, available at https://investmentpolicy.unctad.org/international-investment-agreements/treaty-files/2394/download ("The Arab investor may have recourse to the courts in the State where the investment is made

194. In terms of treaty drafting and taking into account that consent to the jurisdiction of the MIC would be contained in a separate instrument (a future IIA or an existing one for which an opt-in has been exercised),[29] there seem to be two possibilities.

195. First, the MIC Statute may simply defer to any jurisdictional requirements contained in the underlying IIA over which it has jurisdiction. Thus, for instance, where an IIA between States A and B provides for an 18-month litigation requirement, such requirement would continue to apply to proceedings to be brought before the MIC. By contrast, an IIA between States C and D without any such requirement would allow a qualifying investor to directly access the MIC without having to first resort to domestic courts. Under this approach, the MIC Statute would simply defer to any jurisdictional or admissibility requirement (including those aimed at regulating the interplay with domestic courts, including exhaustion, litigation, fork-in-the-road, or waiver clauses) contained in the underlying IIA.

196. An alternative approach would be to include within the MIC *additional* jurisdictional or admissibility requirements to be met in addition to those governing under the IIA. Thus, the MIC Statute could contemplate any of the sequential or alternative methods discussed above, for instance a fork-in-the-road clause, that would apply to *any* proceedings brought before the Court. There would be nothing unusual in this approach; it is adopted by the ICSID Convention, which provides for autonomous jurisdictional requirements (e.g., definition of "investor", nationality restrictions, etc.) which must be met in addition to the conditions set out in the relevant IIA. Further, if the MIC Statute wishes to provide greater flexibility to Contracting States (with a view to reaching a wider consensus), it could leave it to the Contracting States to opt into some but not all of these requirements (like Article 26 of the ICSID Convention for exhaustion of local remedies). For instance, the MIC Statute could provide that no exhaustion of local remedies is required before the Court, unless a Contracting State indicates otherwise when acceding or ratifying the treaty.

197. The role of courts in support and control of the proceedings may considerably change as a result of the transition from arbitration to a standing body, depending on how the MIC is conceived. If, as is likely, the MIC is a self-contained court, governed solely by public international law,[30] the role of domestic courts would be much curtailed:

---

according to the rules of jurisdiction within such State in the case of matters which fall within the jurisdiction of the Court. However, where the Arab investor brings an action before one authority, he must refrain from so doing before the other"; "Where there is a conflict of jurisdiction between the Court and the courts of a State Party, the decision of the Court on the matter shall be final"). See also Hasaan (2019), p. 124 (discussing the 2013 Amendment to the Arab Investment Agreement, noting that such amendment contains a similar fork-in road clause, and discussing relevant cases before the Arab investment Court).

[29]Without prejudice to the possibility for consent to the MIC to be given also in an investment contract between a foreign investor and a State (or State-entity) and through an offer in national legislation. These are policy choices on the jurisdiction of the prospective MIC which are for States to make.

[30]See Gabrielle Kaufmann-Kohler and Michele Potestà (2016), *First CIDS Report*, Section V.5.

- The standing nature of the Court would render any role for domestic courts in the appointment of adjudicators unnecessary.
- With regard to challenges to adjudicators, which are likely to be much less frequent than for arbitrators, the MIC Statute could confer the power to decide on disqualification to an external authority, for instance the PCA Secretary-General, the ICSID Secretary-General, or the ICJ President, or reserve this function to an internal body of the Court.[31]
- In respect of the faculty to seek provisional remedies from domestic courts which may exist under national laws of procedure, the MIC Statute could provide for a solution akin to the one found in the ICSID Convention context, which excludes any such role (unless otherwise provided by the parties).[32]
- The MIC Statute is also likely to provide for its own system of review of first-instance decisions either in the form of an annulment or of an appeal.[33]
- A residual role will remain for domestic courts at the enforcement stage, an issue which these authors analyzed in the First CIDS Report.[34]

4.5 Replacing the Existing System with State-to-State Dispute Settlement

An option that is sometimes discussed is to allow only the home State to enforce the IIA obligations on behalf of their investors through SSDS.[35] This reform option would essentially entail a return to the pre-investment arbitration system of diplomatic protection and resemble the situation under the FCN treaties pre-dating modern BITs. The potential drawbacks of this option have been highlighted in Chap. 2.[36] **198**.

What effect would a reform proposal aimed at strengthening SSDS have on the role of domestic courts? As previously seen, under customary international law, where the home State brings a claim for injury to one of its nationals against another **199**.

[31] Gabrielle Kaufmann-Kohler and Michele Potestà (2017), *CIDS Supplemental Report*, para. 104.

[32] See *supra* at chapter 3.3.3.

[33] See generally Gabrielle Kaufmann-Kohler and Michele Potestà (2016), *First CIDS Report*, section V.D.

[34] See Gabrielle Kaufmann-Kohler and Michele Potestà (2016), *First CIDS Report*, section V.E.

[35] See for recent practice in this respect Australia-Japan EPA (2014); Australia-Malaysia FTA (2012); Australia-New Zealand Investment Protocol (2011); Japan-Philippines EPA (2006); Australia-U.S. FTA (2004); Comprehensive Progressive Agreement for Trans-Pacific Partnership (2018) as between certain countries only (see the side instruments exchanged by New Zealand with a number of treaty parties, e.g. Australia and Peru, which exclude investor-State dispute settlement as between those parties, available at https://www.mfat.govt.nz/en/trade/free-trade-agreements/free-trade-agreements-in-force/cptpp/comprehensive-and-progressive-agreement-for-trans-pacific-partnership-text-and-resources/).

[36] See *supra* at 2.2.2.2 and 2.3.

State (as opposed to a claim for direct injury to itself), the national must first have exhausted all local remedies.[37] In *Italy v. Cuba*, one of the few inter-State cases under a BIT,[38] the tribunal confirmed that the exhaustion rule was a prerequisite for Italy's diplomatic protection claim under the BIT.[39]

200. Thus, a reform option centered around the enhanced prominence of SSDS would entail a greater role for domestic courts. In their treaties, States could, however, waive exhaustion of local remedies as pre-condition to SSDS, or they could conceive of SSDS and domestic courts as alternative fora. The Brazilian model Cooperation and Investment Facilitation Agreements (CIFA), which does not provide for investor-State arbitration, but opts for a framework involving an Ombudsman, a Joint Committee of the Treaty Parties, and SSDS, specifies that if an investor has obtained a domestic court judgment with *res judicata* effect, resort to SSDS under the treaty is foreclosed; if the domestic court litigation is pending, the investor's waiver of domestic court proceedings is a pre-condition to the home State's commencement of SSDS proceedings.[40]

---

[37] See supra at 2.2.2.2.

[38] See *Italian Republic v. Republic of Cuba*, *ad hoc* arbitral tribunal, Interim Award, 15 March 2005; Potestà (2012), pp. 341–347. For the operation of the exhaustion rule in a different context, see Article 295 of the United Nations Conventions on the Law of the Sea (UNCLOS), providing that "[a]ny dispute between States Parties concerning the interpretation or application of this Convention may be submitted to the procedures provided for in this section only after local remedies have been exhausted where this is required by international law". On this see Marotti (2017), pp. 36–62.

[39] See *Italian Republic v. Republic of Cuba*, *ad hoc* arbitral tribunal, Interim Award, 15 March 2005, paras. 88–91.

[40] See Brazilian CFIA Model, Article 24, para. 13(b) ("This paragraph [possibility to resort to State-to-State arbitration for the purposes of seeking the recovering of compensation for "damages caused by the measure in question under the obligations of this Agreement"] shall not be applied to a dispute concerning a particular investor which has been previously resolved and where protection of res judicata applies. If a[n] investor had submitted claims regarding the measure at issue in the Joint Committee to local courts or an arbitration tribunal of the Host State, the arbitration to examine damages can only be initiated after the withdrawal of such claims by the investor in local courts or an arbitration tribunal of the Host State. If after the establishment of the arbitration, the existence of claims in local courts or arbitral tribunals over the contested measure is made known to the arbitrators or the Parties, the arbitration will be suspended", emphasis added). The second part of the rule is akin to a waiver provision examined *supra* at 3.2.2.2. On the Brazilian CFIA Model, see generally Vidigal and Stevens (2018), pp. 475–512; Bernasconi-Osterwalder and Dietrich Brauch (2015), pp. 1–16. Article 24, para. 14(c) of the Brazil-Colombia CFIA (2015) provides that State-to-State arbitral awards are to be treated as though they are judgments rendered by a local court for the purposes of enforcement (similar to what Article 54 ICSID Convention provides for ICSID awards).

4.6 Two Alternative Models: Preliminary Rulings and Complementarity

Beyond the means of coordination to which IIAs typically resort (exhaustion of local remedies, domestic litigation requirements short of exhaustion, fork-in-the-road, and waiver clauses), it may be instructive to address two coordination modes, or "jurisdiction-regulating" norms, existing in other areas of public international law, namely preliminary rulings and complementarity.[41] Could these be transposed to the investment treaty realm? **201.**

A preliminary ruling proceeding is a procedure by which a court refers a decision on a specific issue arising in pending proceedings to another court, normally seeking the interpretation of a legal norm from the other court. The proceedings before the court seeking the ruling are typically suspended pending the determination by the other court, which will usually bind the court requesting it. That court will then incorporate the content of the ruling into its overall resolution of the dispute. **202.**

The most well-known example is the preliminary ruling procedure pursuant to Article 267 of the Treaty on the Functioning of the European Union (ex Article 234 of the Treaty establishing the European Community), whereby a court of a Member State of the European Union may, and in certain instances must, request the CJEU to give a ruling on the interpretation of a question of EU law that arises in an action pending before the Member State court and is unsettled.[42] In the context of the EU, the preliminary ruling procedure was needed to foster the unity of the EU legal order in spite of the decentralized interpretation and application at the national level. It has worked as a powerful tool to ensure the uniform application of EU law and thereby the preservation of the legal unity of the Union.[43] **203.**

The transposition of a preliminary ruling mechanism to investment *arbitration* (i.e. could an investment tribunal seek a preliminary ruling on an unsettled issue of investment law from a permanent body) has been examined elsewhere.[44] Here, in **204.**

---

[41]See generally Shany (2007), pp. 33–36.

[42]See Consolidated version of the Treaty on the Functioning of the European Union ("TFEU"), OJ C 326, 26 October 2012, Article 267. For preliminary ruling procedures in other international courts and tribunals, see Virzo (2011), pp. 285–313.

[43]In the words of the CJEU, "[the] obligation to refer imposed by the third paragraph of Article 234 EC [now Article 267 TFEU] is based on cooperation, *established with a view to ensuring the proper application and uniform interpretation of [EU] law in all the Member States*, between national courts, in their capacity as courts responsible for the application of [EU] law, and the Court of Justice [. . .]". See Case C-495/03 *Intermodal Transports BV v. Staatssecretaris van Financiën* [2005] ECR I-8151, para. 38 (emphasis added). On preliminary rulings in EU law, see generally de la Mare and Donnelly (2011), pp. 363–406.

[44]See Gabrielle Kaufmann-Kohler and Michele Potestà (2016), *First CIDS Report*, Section V.D.4.a (discussing, in the context of a prospective MIC, the possible creation of a panel allowed to refer certain questions to either a separate body established for that purpose or to a special chamber of the MIC). See also generally Kaufmann-Kohler (2004), p. 221; Kaufmann-Kohler (2005), p. 8; Kaufmann-Kohler (2007), p. 378; Schreuer (2006), pp. 23; Schreuer (2008), pp. 207–212; Diel-Gligor (2017).

line with the aim of this study, the purpose is to inquire whether it could be contemplated that a *national court* seized of an issue of international investment law could seek a preliminary ruling from one of the four *international* dispute settlement systems envisaged above (investment arbitration, AM, MIC, SSDS).[45] Or, put differently, assuming a dispute arising out of an IIA is brought before a national court, could that court refer an unsettled question of interpretation of that IIA to an international dispute settlement body? In accordance with the preliminary ruling logic, the international body from which the ruling is requested would not dispose of the dispute pending before the national forum. It would merely authoritatively determine a discrete issue of international investment law to assist the domestic court in resolving the dispute. At the same time, that practice would work toward the "uniformization" of international investment law.

205. While in theory conceivable, the transposition of this model in the investment law setting at issue appears difficult, if only because the governing law before the domestic court would not necessarily be international law. Indeed, as was seen above, in certain legal systems, domestic courts cannot apply IIAs directly as a result of constitutional limitations.[46] Hence, in such a situation, a preliminary ruling mechanism would serve no purpose.

206. An alternative model for the interplay between domestic and international jurisdiction is the principle of complementarity enshrined in the Rome Statute of the International Criminal Court.[47] Under this principle, States have the first responsibility and right to prosecute the most serious crimes of international concern. The International Criminal Court may only exercise jurisdiction where the national legal system "is unwilling or unable genuinely to carry out the investigation or prosecution" (Article 17 of the Rome Statute).[48] Transposed to investment disputes, the international settlement mechanism would exercise a sort of "jurisdiction of last resort"; it would do so in the absence of a credible judicial alternative at the national

[45]See also Schill and Vidigal (2018), p. 19.

[46]See *supra* at 3.2.2.1. See also Freya Baetens (2015), Transatlantic Investment Treaty Protection – A Response to Poulsen, Bonnitcha and Yackee, Paper No. 4 in the CEPS-CTR project "TTIP in the Balance" and CEPS Special Report No. 103 / March 2015, p. 4.

[47]See Rome Statute of the International Criminal Court ("Rome Statute"), 1 July 2002, 2187 UNTS 90, Preamble ("the International Criminal Court established under this Statute shall be complementary to national criminal jurisdiction"), Article 1 (The International Criminal Court "shall be a permanent institution and shall have the power to exercise its jurisdiction over persons for the most serious crimes of international concern, as referred to in this Statute, and shall be complementary to national criminal jurisdictions"), and Article 17 ("[. . .] the Court shall determine that a case is inadmissible where: (a) The case is being investigated or prosecuted by a State which has jurisdiction over it, unless the State is unwilling or unable genuinely to carry out the investigation or prosecution; (b) The case has been investigated by a State which has jurisdiction over it and the State has decided not to prosecute the person concerned, unless the decision resulted from the unwillingness or inability of the State genuinely to prosecute; (c) The person concerned has already been tried for conduct which is the subject of the complaint, and a trial by the Court is not permitted under article 20, paragraph 3; [. . .]").

[48]See generally Stigen (2008), El Zeidy (2008).

level, i.e. when the domestic courts are "unwilling or unable" to adjudicate the dispute. Complementarity may be regarded as having the advantage of strengthening the capabilities of domestic courts while at the same time preserving international remedies for cases where justice cannot be rendered at the national level. This said, the International Criminal Court is built upon a complex interaction between the State Parties, the U.N. Security Council, the Prosecutor, and the other organs of the Court. These actors or their equivalents are largely absent in the adjudication of investment disputes. As a result, the implementation of a jurisdiction of last resort does not appear practically feasible and would at best be fraught with uncertainty.

In conclusion, while the preliminary rulings and the complementarity models make for an interesting coordination of domestic and international jurisdictions, their implant within the investment framework appears either inapposite (preliminary rulings) or not easily implementable (complementarity). **207.**

4.7 Replacing the Existing System with Domestic Courts

Finally, under the most "radical" reform option advanced by certain stakeholders, domestic courts should become the *exclusive* forum for the settlement of investment disputes. As discussed in previous parts of this study, a wholesale return to only domestic remedies should be considered with caution in particular for States where the courts' impartiality and the rule of law might be open to question. **208.**

States wishing to pursue this option would need to either (i) amend their IIAs to eliminate investor-State arbitration and SSDS clauses; or (ii) terminate their IIAs entirely. Under the first option, domestic courts may apply IIAs, if so allowed under their legal system. Under the second option, investment disputes would simply be adjudicated by reference to domestic legal standards. **209.**

Recent State practice provides some examples of the greater role domestic remedies could play in the adjudication of disputes between States and foreign investors. **210.**

South Africa, for instance, which has adopted a policy against investor-State dispute settlement, has "recently reviewed all of its IIAs and terminated most of them".[49] The investment protection regime is now established under domestic law, in particular, the Protection of Investment Act No. 22 of 2015.[50] According to the Act, foreign investors are entitled to the same treatment as that afforded to South African investors in like circumstances, save for certain exceptions.[51] The "domestication" of the investment regime not only applies to substantive protection, **211.**

[49] See Mbengue and Schacherer (2017), p. 442.

[50] South Africa, Protection of Investment Act 2015 (Act 22 of 2015), Government Gazette, 606, No. 39514, 15 December 2015, available at https://investmentpolicy.unctad.org/investment-laws/laws/157/investment-act.

[51] Article 9 of the South Africa, Protection of Investment Act 2015.

it also extends to procedural remedies. The Act does not provide for investor-State arbitration, but only for recourse to domestic courts.[52] The Government may, however, consent to inter-State arbitration with the investor's home State on a case-by-case basis, subject to the exhaustion of local remedies.[53]

212. Some States have followed a different approach, which has been referred to as "selective judicialisation".[54] Under this approach, the treaty excludes from the jurisdiction of the international tribunal certain "sensitive areas" which are reserved for domestic courts. For instance, the 2015 Indian Model BIT excludes from the scope of the treaty any measure by a local government (as well as any law or measure regarding taxation), compulsory licenses granted in relation to intellectual property, government procurement, subsidies or grants and services supplied in the exercise of governmental authority.[55] As a consequence, disputes arising out of measures of this nature cannot be resolved through the settlement mechanisms foreseen in the treaty and must be brought before national courts.[56]

References

Bernasconi-Osterwalder N, Dietrich Brauch M (2015) Comparative commentary to Brazil's cooperation and investment facilitation agreements (CIFAs) with Mozambique, Angola, Mexico and Malawi. International Institute for Sustainable Development, pp 1–16

de la Mare T, Donnelly C (2011) Preliminary rulings and EU legal integration: evolution and stasis. In: Craig P, de Búrca G (eds) The evolution of EU law, 2nd edn. Oxford University Press, pp 363–406

Diel-Gligor K (2017) Towards consistency in international investment jurisprudence. A preliminary ruling system for ICSID arbitration. Brill | Nijhoff

El Zeidy MM (2008) The principle of complementarity in international criminal law: origin, development and practice. Martinus Nijhoff

Hasaan AA (2019) The 2013 amendments to the Arab Investment Agreement. ICSID Rev Foreign Invest Law J 34:107–135. pp. 1–29

Jansen Calamita N (2017) The (in)compatibility of appellate mechanisms with existing instruments of the investment treaty regime. J World Invest Trade 18(4):585–627

---

[52] Article 13, para. 4 of the South Africa, Protection of Investment Act 2015.

[53] Article 13, para. 5 of the South Africa, Protection of Investment Act 2015.

[54] See Schill and Vidigal (2018), p. 4.

[55] India Model BIT (2015), Article 2, para. 2.4.

[56] For a similar approach, see Comprehensive Progressive Agreement for Trans-Pacific Partnership (2018), Article 29.5 in relation to tobacco control measures, which allows a Contracting State to deny benefits with respect to such claims and specifying that "[s]uch a claim shall not be submitted to arbitration under Section B of Chapter 9 (Investment) if a Party has made such an election". This provision is however without prejudice to "a Party's rights under Chapter 28 (Dispute Settlement) in relation to a tobacco control measure" (see footnote 11) (i.e. SSDS). The United States-Mexico--Canada Agreement (USMCA), Chapter 14 Appendix 2, carves out from the jurisdiction of investor-State tribunals disputes arising from State measures taken to reduce tobacco consumption or debt restructuring.

Kaufmann-Kohler G (2004) Annulment of ICSID awards in contract and treaty arbitrations: are there differences? In: Gaillard E, Banifatemi Y (eds) Annulment of ICSID awards: the foundation of a new investment protection regime in treaty arbitration. IAI Series, No. 1. JurisNet, pp 189–221

Kaufmann-Kohler G (2005) In search of transparency and consistency: ICSID reform proposal. Transnl Disp Manag 2(5):8

Kaufmann-Kohler G (2007) Arbitral precedent: dream, necessity or excuse? The 2006 Freshfields lecture. Arbitr Int 23(3):357–378

Kaufmann-Kohler G, Rigozzi A (2015) International arbitration law and practice in Switzerland. Oxford University Press, p 528

Marotti L (2017) Determining the scope of the local remedies rule in UNCLOS disputes. In: Lachenmann F, Wolfrum R (eds) Max Planck Yearbook of United Nations law, vol 21. Brill | Nijhoff, pp 36–62

Mbengue MM, Schacherer S (2017) The 'Africanization' of international investment law: the Pan-African investment code and the reform of the international investment regime. J World Invest Trade 18(3):414–448

McGarry B, Ostřanský J (2017) Is the law of treaties an obstacle or a conduit for the reform of investor-state dispute settlement? Emory Int Law Rev 32:1001–1013

Potestà M (2012) Republic of Italy v. Republic of Cuba. Am J Int Law 106:341–347

Potestà M (2015) Towards a greater role for state-to-state arbitration in the architecture of investment treaties? In: Lalani S, Polanco R (eds) The role of the state in investor-state arbitration. Brill | Nijhoff, pp 249–273

Roberts A (2018) Incremental, systemic, and paradigmatic reform of investor-state arbitration. Am J Int law 112(3):410–432

Schill SW, Vidigal G (2018) Cutting the Gordian Knot: Investment Dispute Settlement à la Carte. RTA Exchange, Geneva International Centre for Trade and Sustainable Development and the Inter-America Development Bank, p 19

Schreuer CH (2006) Diversity and harmonization of treaty interpretation in investment arbitration. Transnl Disp Manag 3(2):23

Schreuer CH (2008) Preliminary rulings in investment arbitration. In: Sauvant K (ed) Appeals mechanism in international investment disputes. Oxford University Press, pp 207–212

Shany Y (2007) Regulating jurisdictional relations between National and International Courts. Oxford University Press, pp 27–77

Stigen J (2008) The relationship between the International Criminal Court and National Jurisdictions: the principle of complementarity. Brill | Nijhoff

van den Berg AJ (2019) Appeal mechanisms for ISDS awards: interaction with New York and ICSID Conventions. In: Asian Academy of International Law's proceedings ISDS reform conference 2019, mapping the way forward, Hong Kong SAR, China, (13 February 2019), pp 104–107

Vidigal G, Stevens B (2018) Brazil's new model of dispute settlement for investment: return to the past or alternative for the future? J World Invest Trade 19:475–512

Virzo R (2011) The preliminary ruling procedures at international regional courts and tribunals. Law Prac Int Courts Tribunals 10(2):285–313

Chapter 5
Conclusions and Recommendations

This study has sought to analyze the relationship between national and international courts in the field of foreign investment protection as it arises from the extensive investment treaty framework built by States over the last five decades. It has also suggested possible modes for regulating jurisdictional interactions under various dispute settlement scenarios that may emerge in the coming years. **213**

To that end, it has first recalled why investment arbitration was created: to depoliticize dispute resolution and do away with the constraints of diplomatic protection, to attract foreign capital, and to offer an alternative to local courts.[1] Since the creation of investment arbitration (now over five decades ago), economic and political power has shifted considerably from traditionally high-income economies to emerging ones. Numerous new economic partnerships have also emerged beyond the traditional North-South (or developed-developing country) divisions. In the field of dispute resolution, investment disputes are no longer brought solely against developing or emerging economies, but also against traditionally capital-exporting States. Global concerns have evolved, too. While the attraction of foreign capital and the protection of nationals investing abroad remain notable objectives for many States, they must now be coordinated with sustainable development goals, which require strong policies for the protection of the environment, public health, human rights, among other public goods. The enforcement of these policies may well require adjustments in the balance between investment protection and regulatory powers, and a recalibration of the substantive standards can already be observed in many recent treaties. **214**

Against the backdrop of these evolutions, the continuing need for international mechanisms allowing foreign investors to bring claims against sovereign States for violations of investment standards of protection is at times questioned. In the eyes of critics, the IIA investment arbitration regime does not account for situations in which **215**

[1]See *supra* at Chap. 2.

G. Kaufmann-Kohler, M. Potestà, *Investor-State Dispute Settlement and National Courts*, European Yearbook of International Economic Law,
https://doi.org/10.1007/978-3-030-44164-7_5

domestic courts *do* offer adequate access to justice and discriminates against domestic investors by granting only (certain) foreign investors a privileged procedural track. While these are valid questions that States and all other stakeholders should continuously assess and re-assess, this study has shown that there are good reasons to maintain an international mechanism to settle investment disputes to which private parties have direct access; it is certainly another issue what form (or forms) this mechanism should take. In a nutshell, the reasons include the importance of giving investors signals that inspire confidence and enhance credibility, including by providing them with a neutral forum distinct from the host State's judicial system, which may be perceived, rightly or wrongly, as not entirely impartial. Furthermore, in considering whether to maintain some form of international dispute settlement mechanism with direct claims, the alternatives must be carefully weighed, in particular in terms of the consequences of a return to diplomatic protection for investors, home States and host States.[2]

216 The determination of the future function of international investment dispute settlement bodies may well vary depending on each State's role as capital exporter, capital importer, protector of its nationals investing abroad, and potential respondent against claims brought by foreign investors. The answer for each State may also be contingent on the particular treaty partner it faces in a specific IIA negotiation. It may also hinge on whether the negotiating States share common legal traditions and comparable cultural histories, and/or place mutual trust in each other's institutions, in particular the judiciary.

217 With these considerations in mind, the study has examined the many facets of the interaction between domestic courts and an international dispute settlement mechanism for investment disputes, from peaceful coexistence and support in the context of supervisory powers, to possible conflicts and tensions when two adjudicatory bodies rule on the same State measure.[3] This potential for conflict is due to the multiplicity of legal bases on which a given State measure can be challenged, including national constitutional, administrative, contract, tax law, and international investment law. It is further due to the fact that each of these legal bases or regimes has its own procedural remedies. In some instances, the plurality of proceedings may serve legitimate purposes, for instance when the relief sought is different and not conflicting. However, in other cases, it may be essentially duplicative and thus a waste of resources, both public and private.

218 In those circumstances, it may not be sustainable in the long run to ignore the problems presented by concurrent domestic and international proceedings concerning the same measure. Treaty negotiators have thus appropriately designed tools to avoid these wasteful duplications, mainly in the form of fork-in-the-road and waiver clauses. The diverse solutions examined in Sect. 3.2 of this study are based on different philosophies and each presents advantages and disadvantages. No single model of regulation exists, and different types of regulations may respond to

---

[2]See *supra* at Chap. 2.3.

[3]See *supra* at Chap. 3.

different State needs and policies. Whatever the States' individual preferences, these clauses could be improved in order to better capture certain undesirable consequences arising from duplicative proceedings.

Finally, this study has mapped out the possible interplay between domestic courts 219
and international dispute settlement mechanisms in the possible reform scenarios that are being considered by States.[4] States wishing to keep the current framework based on *ad hoc* arbitration, perhaps improved through targeted, incremental reforms, may consider the possibility of including rules on the coordination of domestic and international proceedings analyzed in this paper and subject to possible improvements, as previously mentioned. Furthermore, States wishing to transition toward greater institutionalization of the dispute resolution framework, such as by the creation of an AM or a MIC, will need to similarly examine the relationship between those new international bodies and domestic courts, as opportunities for judicial dialogue, overlaps, and even tensions will not disappear in more institutionalized frameworks. The prospective creation of such institutions would also require revisiting the role of domestic courts in relation to the international mechanism, in particular but not exclusively the courts' functions in supervising the international process. That role would have to be adapted to the changed dispute settlement framework.

In conclusion, what emerges from this study is an investment protection system 220
for which domestic and international court and tribunals share responsibilities in many and sometimes quite elaborate ways. The system has grown over time, organically so to say. The result is that, in certain areas of the interactions, the allocation of tasks is not always optimal and inefficiencies burden the system. In these areas, there is a need for improvement by providing for a more fruitful work division among domestic and international dispute settlement bodies. Whether or not reforms are implemented and whatever their format, the end goal should be a more efficient and just international dispute settlement system that achieves a fair balance between the private interests of the investors and the public interest represented by the States.

[4] See *supra* at Chap. 4.

Legal Texts and Other Materials

United Nations

International Law Commission (2006), *Draft Articles on Diplomatic Protection with commentaries*, Report of the Fifty-Eighth Session, UN Doc. A/61/10, 2006/II(2) ILC Yearbook.

International Law Commission (2006), *Draft Articles on Diplomatic Protection,* Official Records of the General Assembly, Sixty-first Session, Supplement No. 10, UN Doc. A/61/10.

James Crawford (Special Rapporteur) (1999), International Law Commission, Second Report on State Responsibility, UN Doc. A/CN.4/498.

UN General Assembly, Report of the United Nations Commission on International Trade Law (Fiftieth Session (3-21 July 2017)), Official Records of the Seventy-second Session, Supplement No. 17 (A/72/17).

UNCITRAL WGIII (Investor-State Dispute Settlement Reform) on the work of its thirty-sixth session (Vienna, 29 October-2 November 2018), *Possible reform of investor-State dispute settlement (ISDS)*—Note by the Secretariat, U.N. Doc. No. A/CN.9/WG.III/WP.142.

UNCITRAL WGIII (Investor-State Dispute Settlement Reform) on the work of its thirty-sixth session (Vienna, 29 October–2 November 2018), *Possible reform of investor-State dispute settlement (ISDS)—Note by the Secretariat*, A/CN.9/WG.III/WP.149.

UNCITRAL WGIII (Investor-State Dispute Settlement Reform) on the work of its thirty-sixth session (Vienna, 29 October–2 November 2018), *Possible reform of investor-State dispute settlement (ISDS) Consistency and related matters - Note by the Secretariat*, A/CN.9/WG.III/WP.150.

UNCITRAL WGIII (Investor-State Dispute Settlement Reform) on the work of its thirty-sixth session (Vienna, 29 October–2 November 2018), *Possible reform of investor-State dispute settlement (ISDS) Ensuring independence and impartiality on*

G. Kaufmann-Kohler, M. Potestà, *Investor-State Dispute Settlement and National Courts*, European Yearbook of International Economic Law,
https://doi.org/10.1007/978-3-030-44164-7

the part of arbitrators and decision makers in ISDS - Note by the Secretariat, A/CN.9/WG.III/WP.151.

UNCITRAL WGIII (Investor-State Dispute Settlement Reform) on the work of its thirty-sixth session (Vienna, 29 October–2 November 2018), *Possible reform of investor-State dispute settlement (ISDS) Arbitrators and decision makers: appointment mechanisms and related issues—Note by the Secretariat*, A/CN.9/WG.III/WP.152.

UNCITRAL WGIII (Investor-State Dispute Settlement Reform) on the work of its thirty-sixth session (Vienna, 29 October–2 November 2018), *Possible reform of investor-State dispute settlement (ISDS) Cost and duration - Note by the Secretariat*, A/CN.9/WG.III/WP.153.

UNCITRAL WGIII (Investor-State Dispute Settlement Reform) on the work of its thirty-seventh session (New York, 1–5 April 2019), *Possible reform of investor-State dispute settlement (ISDS): Third-party funding—Note by the Secretariat*, A/CN.9/WG.III/WP.157.

UNCTAD (2014), IIA Issue Note—Working Draft, *The Impact of IIA on FDI: an overview of empirical studies 1998–2014*.

UNCTAD (2015), World Investment Report 2015—Reforming International Investment Governance, available at https://unctad.org/en/PublicationsLibrary/wir2015_en.pdf.

UNCTAD (2018), World Investment Report, Investment and New Industrial Policies, available at https://unctad.org/en/PublicationsLibrary/wir2018_en.pdf.

UNCTAD (2019), *Fact Sheet on Investor-State Dispute Settlement Cases in 2018*, IIA Issues Note on International Investment Agreements No 2, May 2019.

European Union

European Commission (2019), *The 2019 EU Justice Scoreboard*, May 2019, COM (2019) 198/2.

European Parliament (2011), Resolution of 6 April 2011 on the Future European International Investment Policy (2010/2203(INI)), P7_TA (2011)0141.

European Parliament (2015) Opinion of the Committee on Legal Affairs for the Committee on International Trade on recommendations to the European Commission on the negotiations for the Transatlantic Trade and Investment Partnership (2014/2228INI)), 4 May 2015, Rapporteur Dietmar Köster.

Opinion of the European Committee of the Regions (2015), 110th Plenary Session, 11–13 February 2015, (2015/C 140/02), 28 April 2015.

Opinion 1/17 EU Canada Comprehensive Economic and Trade Agreement [2019] ECLI:EU:C:2019:341.

ICSID

ICSID Model Clauses, available at http://icsidfiles.worldbank.org/icsid/icsid/staticfiles/model-clauses-en/14.htm.

ICSID (1968), *History of the ICSID Convention: Documents Concerning the Origin and Formulation of the Convention on the Settlement of Investment Disputes between States and Nationals of Other States*, ICSID, Vol.II-1.

Report of the Executive Directors on the Convention on the Settlement of Investment Disputes Between States and Nationals of Other States, Section III, 18 March 1965.

ICSID (2019), *Contracting States and Measures Taken By Them For The Purpose Of The Convention*, Doc. ICSID/8, February 2019, available at https://icsid.worldbank.org/en/Documents/icsiddocs/ICSID%208-Contracting%20States%20and%20Measures%20Taken%20by%20Them%20for%20the%20Purpose%20of%20the%20Convention.pdf.

ICSID (2019), *The ICSID Caseload – Statistics,* Issue 2019-2, p. 7 available at https://icsid.worldbank.org/en/Documents/ICSID_Web_Stats_2019-2_(English).pdf.

OECD

OECD, Government Perspectives on Investor-State Dispute Settlement: A Progress Report, 14 December 2012, p. 7, available at https://www.oecd.org/daf/inv/investment-policy/ISDSprogressreport.pdf.

World Economic Forum

Klaus Schwab (2018), *World Economic Forum The Global Competitiveness Report,* available at http://www3.weforum.org/docs/GCR2018/05FullReport/TheGlobalCompetitivenessReport2018.pdf.

Asian Development Bank

Asian Development Bank (2016), *ASEAN Economic Integration Report 2016.*

References

Allee T, Peinhardt C (2011) Contingent credibility: the impact of investment treaty violations on foreign direct investment. Int Organ 65(3):401–432

Allen BE, Soave T (2014) Jurisdictional overlap in WTO dispute settlement and investment arbitration. Arbitr Int 30(1):1–58

Armstrong S, Nottage L (2016) The impact of investment treaties and ISDS provisions on foreign direct investment: a baseline econometric analysis, Sydney Law School Legal Studies Research Paper No. 16/74 (August 2016)

Armstrong A, Winkler J (2017) Foreign investment and shared sovereignty, National Institute of Economic and Social Research Discussion Paper No. 475 (July 2017)

Berger A, Busse M, Nunnenkamp P, Roy M (2011) More stringent BITs, less ambiguous effects on FDI? Not a BIT! Econ Lett 112:270–272

Berger A, Busse M, Nunnenkamp P, Roy M (2013) Do trade and investment agreements lead to more FDI? Accounting for key provisions inside the black box. Int Econ Econ Policy 10 (2):248–275

Bernardini P (2010) ICSID versus non-ICSID investment treaty arbitration. In: Fernández-Ballesteros MA, Lozano DA (eds) Liber Amicorum Bernardo Cremades. Wolters Kluwer, Alphen aan den Rijn, pp 159–188

Bernasconi-Osterwalder N, Brauch MD (2015) Comparative commentary to Brazil's Cooperation and Investment Facilitation Agreements (CIFAs) with Mozambique, Angola, Mexico and Malawi. International Institute for Sustainable Development, Winnipeg, pp 1–16

Besson S (2016) Droit international public, 3rd edn. Stämpfli Verlag AG, Bern, pp 333–337

Bjorklund AK (2004) Waiver and the exhaustion of local remedies rule in NAFTA jurisprudence. In: Weiler T (ed) NAFTA investment law and arbitration: past issues, current practice, future prospects. Brill|Nijhoff, Leiden, pp 253–286

Bjorklund AK (2007) Private rights and public international law: why competition among international economic tribunals is not working. Hastings Law J 59:241–308

Bonnitcha J, Skovgaard Poulsen LN, Waibel M (2017) The political economy of the investment treaty regime. Oxford University Press, Oxford

Brauch MD (2017) Exhaustion of local remedies in international investment law. International Institute for Sustainable Development, Winnipeg, Best Practices Series

Broches A (1995) Settlement of investment disputes, address to the world conference on world peace through law. In: Broches A (ed) Selected essays: World Bank, ICSID, and other subjects of public and private international law. Martinus Nijhoff, Leiden

G. Kaufmann-Kohler, M. Potestà, *Investor-State Dispute Settlement and National Courts*, European Yearbook of International Economic Law,
https://doi.org/10.1007/978-3-030-44164-7

Bronckers M (2015) Is Investor–State Dispute Settlement (ISDS) superior to litigation before domestic courts? An EU view on bilateral trade agreements. J Int Econ Law 18:655–677

Brower CN, Goodman REM (1991) Provisional measures and the protection of ICSID jurisdictional exclusivity against municipal proceedings. ICSID Rev Foreign Invest Law J 6 (2):431–461

Büthe T, Milner HV (2008) The politics of foreign direct investment into developing countries: increasing FDI through international trade agreements? Am J Political Sci 52(4):741–762

Büthe T, Milner HV (2014) Foreign direct investment and institutional diversity in trade agreements: credibility, commitment, and economic flows in the developing world, 1971–2007. World Politics 66(1):88–122

Calamita NJ (2015) The rule of law, investment treaties and economic growth: mapping normative and empirical questions. In: Jowell J, Thomas JC, van Zyl Smit J (eds) Rule of law symposium 2014: the importance of rule of law in promoting development. Singapore Academy of Law and Bingham Centre for the Rule of Law, Singapore, pp 103–128

Calamita NJ (2017) The (In)compatibility of appellate mechanisms with existing instruments of the investment treaty regime. J World Invest Trade 18(4):585–627

Chaisse J, Bellak C (2011) Do bilateral investment treaties promote foreign direct investment? Preliminary reflections on a new methodology. Transnational Corp Rev 3(4):3–10

Chaisse J, Bellak C (2015) Navigating the expanding universe of international treaties on foreign investment creation and use of a critical index. J Int Econ Law 18:79–115

Collins L (1992-III) Provisional and protective measures in international litigation. In: Recueil des Cours 218, vol 234

Crawford J (2008) Treaty and contract in investment arbitration. Arbitr Int 24(3):351–374

Crawford J, Grant TD (2007) Local remedies, exhaustion of. In: Wolfrum R (ed) Max Planck Encyclopedia of Public International Law. Oxford University Press, Oxford

de la Mare T, Donnelly C (2011) Preliminary rulings and EU legal integration: evolution and stasis. In: Craig P, de Búrca G (eds) The evolution of EU law, 2nd edn. Oxford University Press, Oxford, pp 363–406

De Luca A (2016) Direct effect of EU's investment agreements and the Energy Charter Treaty in the EU, Rivista Eurojus.it, 15 November 2016, Available at http://rivista.eurojus.it/direct-effect-of-eus-investment-agreements-and-the-energy-charter-treaty-in-the-eu/

Delaume GR (1983) ICSID arbitration and the courts. Am J Int Law 77(4):784–803

Delaume GR (1984) ICSID arbitration in practice. Int Tax Bus Lawyer 2:58–78

Demirkol B (2018) Judicial acts and investment treaty arbitration. Cambridge University Press, Cambridge

Desbordes R (2017) A granular approach to the effects of bilateral investment treaties and regional trade investment agreements on foreign direct investment, ABD Working Paper

Diel-Gligor K (2017) Towards consistency in international investment jurisprudence. A preliminary ruling system for ICSID arbitration. Brill|Nijhoff, Leiden

Dodge WS (2006) Investor-state dispute settlement between developed countries: reflections on the Australia-United States free trade agreement. Vanderbilt J Transnational Law 39(1):1–37

Dolzer R, Schreuer C (2008) Principles of international investment law, 1st edn. Oxford University Press, Oxford

Dolzer R, Schreuer CH (2012) Principles of international investment law, 2nd edn. Oxford University Press, Oxford

Douglas Z (2004) The hybrid foundations of investment treaty arbitration. Br Yearb Int Law 74 (1):151–289

Douglas Z (2012) The international law of investment claims. Cambridge University Press, Cambridge

Douglas Z (2014) International responsibility for domestic adjudication: denial of justice deconstructed. Int Comp Law Q 63(4):867–900

El Zeidy MM (2008) The principle of complementarity in international criminal law: origin, development and practice. Martinus Nijhoff, Leiden

Fix-Fierro H, López-Ayllón S (1997) The impact of globalization on the reform of the state and the law in Latin America. Houston J Int Law 19(3):785–801

Franck S (2019) Arbitration costs, myths and realities in investment treaty arbitration. Oxford University Press, Oxford

Frenkel M, Walter B (2019) Do bilateral investment treaties attract foreign direct investment? The role of international dispute settlement provisions. World Econ 42(5):1316–1342

Friedland PD (1986) Provisional measures and ICSID arbitration. Arbitr Int 2(4):335–357

Galbraith J (2019) Contemporary practice of the United States relating to international law, NAFTA is renegotiated and signed by the United States. Am J Int Law 113(1):150–159

García-Castrillón CO (2016) Spain and investment arbitration: the renewable energy explosion, investor-state arbitration series, Paper No. 17, November 2016. Centre for International Governance Innovation

Gaukrodger D (2018) Appointing authorities and the selection of arbitrators in investor-state dispute settlement: an overview, OECD Consultation Paper, March 2018, paras. 205–222, available at http://www.oecd.org/investment/investment-policy/ISDS-Appointing-Authorities-Arbitration-March-2018.pdf

Gertz G, Jandhyala S, Skovgaard Poulsen LN (2018) Legalization, diplomacy, and development: do investment treaties de-politicize investment disputes? World Dev 107:238–252

Gil R (2009) ICSID provisional measures to enjoin parallel domestic litigation. World Arbitr Mediation Rev 3(4–5):353–602

Ginsburg T (2005) International substitutes for domestic institutions: bilateral investment treaties and governance. Int Rev Law Econ 25(1):107–123

Giroud S (2012) Enforcement against state assets and execution of ICSID awards in Switzerland: how Swiss Courts deal with immunity defences. ASA Bull 4:758–766

Guthrie BK (2013) Beyond investment protection: an examination of the potential influence of investment treaties on domestic rule of law. New York Univ J Int Law Politics 45:1152–1200

Hallward-Driemeier M (2003) Do bilateral investment treaties attract FDI? Only a bit. . .and they could bite, World Bank, Policy Research Paper WPS 3121

Hanessian G, Duggal K (2017) The final 2015 Indian Model BIT: is this the change the world wishes to see? ICSID Rev Foreign Invest Law J 32(1):216–226

Hasaan AA (2019) The 2013 amendments to the Arab Investment Agreement. ICSID Rev Foreign Invest Law J 34:107–135. pp. 1–29

Hathaway OA, McElroy S, Solow SA (2012) International law at home: enforcing treaties in U.S. Courts. Yale J Int Law 37(1):51–106

Hepburn J (2009) India agrees new investment treaty text with Colombia, Belarus and Taiwan, advancing some of its key concerns such as partial exhaustion and human rights [Updated], IAReporter, (1 January 2019)

Hepburn J (2015) Uzan family may return to ICSID, as Switzerland reveals details of threatened investor claim, IAReporter, 17 March 2015

Hober K, Eliasson N (2018) Review of non-ICSID awards by National Courts. In: Yannaca-Small K (ed) Arbitration under international investment agreements, a guide to the key issues, 2nd edn. Oxford University Press, Oxford

John TS (2018) The rise of investor-state arbitration: politics, law, and unintended consequences. Oxford University Press, Oxford

Johnson L (2015) Aligning Swiss investment treaties with sustainable development: an assessment of current policy coherence and options for future action. Columbia Centre on Sustainable Investment, New York

Johnson L, Volkov O (2013) Investor-state contracts, host-state "Commitments" and the myth of stability in international law. Am Rev Int Arbitr 24(3):361–415

Johnson L, Sachs L, Güven B, Coleman J (2018) Clearing the path: withdrawal of consent and termination as next steps for reforming international investment law, Columbia Center on Sustainable Development Policy Paper, April 2018

Kaiser K (2013) Treaties, direct applicability. In: Wolfrum R (ed) Max Planck encyclopedia of public international law, 2nd edn. Oxford University Press, Oxford

Kalderimis D (2016) The authority of investment treaty tribunals to issue orders restraining domestic court proceedings. ICSID Rev Foreign Invest Law J 31(3):549–575

Kaufmann-Kohler G (2004) Annulment of ICSID awards in contract and treaty arbitrations: are there differences? In: Gaillard E, Banifatemi Y (eds) Annulment of ICSID awards: the foundation of a new investment protection regime in treaty arbitration, IAI Series, No. 1. JurisNet, Huntington, pp 189–221

Kaufmann-Kohler G (2005) In search of transparency and consistency: ICSID reform proposal. Transnational Dispute Manag 2(5):1–8

Kaufmann-Kohler G (2007) Arbitral precedent: dream, necessity or excuse?, The 2006 Freshfields lecture. Arbitr Int 23(3):357–378

Kaufmann-Kohler G (2013) Commercial arbitration before international court and tribunals – reviewing abusive conduct of domestic courts. Arbitr Int 29(2):153–174

Kaufmann-Kohler G, Potestà M (2016) Can the Mauritius convention serve as a model for the reform of investor-State arbitration in connection with the introduction of a permanent investment tribunal or an appeal mechanism? Analysis and Roadmap, CIDS Report, 3 June 2016

Kaufmann-Kohler G, Potestà M (2017) The composition of a multilateral investment court and of an appeal mechanism for investment awards, CIDS Supplemental Report, 15 November 2017

Kaufmann-Kohler G, Rigozzi A (2015) International arbitration law and practice in Switzerland. Oxford University Press, Oxford

Kaufmann-Kohler G, Antonietti A, Potestà M (2018) Interim relief in investment arbitration. In: Yannaca-Small K (ed) Arbitration under international investment agreements, a guide to the key issues, 2nd edn. Oxford University Press, Oxford

Kawharu A, Nottage L (2018) Renouncing investor-state dispute settlement in Australia, then New Zealand: Déjà vu, The University of Sydney Law School Legal Studies Research Paper Series No. 18/03 (February 2018)

Kerner A (2009) Why should I believe you? The costs and consequences of bilateral investment treaties. Int Stud Q 53(1):73–102

Kjos HE (2016) International law through the national prism: the role of domestic law and jurisprudence in shaping international investment law. In: Reinisch A, Footer ME, Binder C (eds) International law and . . .: select proceedings of the European Society of International Law. Hart Publishing, New York, pp 81–96

Kleinheisterkamp J (2012) Investment protection and EU law: the intra- and extra-EU dimension of the Energy Charter Treaty. J Int Econ Law 15(1):85–109

Kriebaum U (2009) Local remedies and the standards for the protection of foreign investment. In: Binder C, Kriebaum U, Reinisch A, Wittich S (eds) International investment law for the 21st century. Oxford University Press, Oxford, pp 417–462

Kriebaum U (2018) Evaluating social benefits and costs of investment treaties: depoliticization of investment disputes. ICSID Rev Foreign Invest Law J 33(1):14–28

Marotti L (2017) Determining the scope of the local remedies rule in UNCLOS disputes. In: Lachenmann F, Wolfrum R (eds) Max Planck Yearbook of United Nations law, vol 21. Brill| Nijhoff, Leiden, pp 36–62

Maurer N (2013) The empire trap. The rise and fall of U.S. intervention to protect American property overseas, 1893–2013. Princeton University Press, Princeton

Mbengue MM, Schacherer S (2017) The 'Africanization' of international investment law: the Pan-African investment code and the reform of the international investment regime. J World Invest Trade 18(3):414–448

McGarry B, Ostřanský J (2017) Is the law of treaties an obstacle or a conduit for the reform of investor-state dispute settlement? Emory Int Law Rev 32:1001–1013

Miles K (2013) The origins of international investment law: empire, environment and the safeguarding of capital. Cambridge University Press, Cambridge

Mourre A, Vagenheim A (2010) Some comments on denial of justice in public and private international law after Loewen and Saipem. In: Fernández-Ballesteros MA, Lozano DA (eds) Liber Amicorum Bernardo Cremades. Wolters Kluwer, Alphen aan den Rijn, pp 843–866
Muchlinski P (2009) Diplomatic protection of foreign investments. In: Binder C, Kriebaum U, Reinisch A, Wittich S (eds) International investment law for the 21st century. Oxford University Press, Oxford
Neumayer E, Spess L (2005) Do bilateral investment treaties increase foreign direct investment to developing countries? World Dev 33(10):1567–1585
Newcombe A, Paradell L (2009) Law and practice of investment treaties: standards of treatment. Wolters Kluwer, Alphen aan den Rijn
Orrego Vicuña F (2004) International dispute settlement in an evolving global society: constitutionalization, accessibility, privatization (Hersch Lauterpacht Memorial Lectures 2001 – Lauterpacht Research Centre for International Law University of Cambridge). Cambridge University Press, Cambridge
Ortiz AL, Ugalde-Revilla P, Chinn C (2016) The role of national courts in ICSID arbitration. In: Baltag C (ed) ICSID Convention after 50 years: unsettled issues. Wolters Kluwer, Alphen aan den Rijn, pp 329–362
Paparinskis M (2010) The limits of depoliticisation in contemporary investor-state arbitration. In: Crawford J, Nouwen S (eds) Select proceedings of the European Society of International Law, vol 3. Hart Publishing, Oxford, pp 271–282
Parra AR (1993) The practices and experience of ICSID. In: ICC, conservatory and provisional measures in international arbitration, ICC Publication No. 519, pp 37–44
Parra AR (2012) The history of ICSID. Oxford University Press, Oxford
Parvanov PP, Kantor M (2012) Comparing U.S. law and recent U.S. investment agreements: much more similar than you might expect. In: Sauvant KP (ed) Yearbook on international investment law & policy 2010–2011. Oxford University Press, Oxford
Paulsson J (2005) Denial of justice in international law. Cambridge University Press, Cambridge
Pauwelyn J (2014) At the edge of chaos? Foreign investment law as a complex adaptive system, how it emerged and how it can be reformed. ICSID Rev Foreign Invest Law J 29(2):372–418
Pearsall P (2018) The role of the state and the ISDS trinity. AJIL Unbound 112:249–254
Peinhardt C, Allee T (2012) Devil in the details? The investment effects of dispute settlement variation in BITs. In: Sauvant K (ed) Yearbook on international investment law & policy 2010–2011. Oxford University Press, Oxford, pp 401–432
Pohl J (2018) Societal benefits and costs of international investment agreements: a critical review of aspects and available empirical evidence, OECD Working Papers on International Investment, No. 2018/1
Pohl J, Mashigo K, Nohen A (2012) Dispute settlement provisions in international investment agreements: a large sample survey, OECD working papers on international investment, 2012/02. OECD Publishing, Paris
Porterfield M (2015) Exhaustion of local remedies in investor-state dispute settlement: an idea whose time has come? Yale J Int Law 41:1–12
Potestà M (2012) Republic of Italy v. Republic of Cuba. Am J Int Law 106:341–347
Potestà M (2015) Towards a greater role for state-to-state arbitration in the architecture of investment treaties? In: Lalani S, Polanco R (eds) The role of the state in investor-state arbitration. Brill|Nijhoff, Leiden, pp 249–273
Price DM (2000) Some observations on chapter eleven of NAFTA. Hastings Int Comp Law Rev 23:421–429
Price DM (2011) Chapter 11 – private party vs. government, investor-state dispute settlement: Frankenstein or safety valve? Canada U S Law J 26:107–114
Puig S (2013) Investor-state tribunals and constitutional courts: the Mexican Sweeteners Saga. Mexican Law Rev 5(2):199–243
Radicati di Brozolo L, Malintoppi L (2010) Unlawful interference with International Arbitration by National Courts of the Seat in the Aftermath of Saipem v. Bangladesh. In: Fernández-

Ballesteros MA, Lozano DA (eds) Liber Amicorum Bernardo Cremades. Wolters Kluwer, Alphen aan den Rijn, pp 993–1012

Radjai N, Stirnimann FX (2013) Investment arbitration. In: Arroyo M (ed) Arbitration in Switzerland – the practitioner's guide: commentary. Wolters Kluwer, Alphen aan den Rijn, pp 1049–1112

Ranjan P, Anand P (2017) The 2016 model Indian bilateral investment treaty: a critical deconstruction. Northwestern J Int Law Bus 38(1):1–55

Reinisch A (2018) Enforcement of investment treaty awards. In: Yannaca-Small K (ed) Arbitration under international investment agreements, a guide to the key issues, 2nd edn. Oxford University Press, Oxford

Roberts A (2018) Incremental, systemic, and paradigmatic reform of investor-state arbitration. Am J Int Law 112(3):410–432

Sattorova M (2018) The impact of investment treaty law on host states: enabling good governance? Hart Publishing, Oxford

Scherer M, Murphy L (2019) Inventory of arbitration proceedings based on Swiss Bilateral Investment Treaties (BIT) (Update 2018). ASA Bull 37(1):9–26

Scherer M, Heiskanen V, Moss S (2009) Domestic review of investment treaty arbitration: the Swiss experience. ASA Bull 27(2):256–279

Schill SW (2009) The multilateralization of international investment law. Cambridge University Press, Cambridge

Schill SW (2010) Private enforcement of international investment law: why we need investor standing in BIT dispute settlement. In: Waibel M, Kaushal A, Chung K-HL, Balchin C (eds) The Backlash against investment arbitration. Wolters Kluwer, Alphen aan den Rijn, pp 29–50

Schill SW (2015) International investment law and the rule of law. In: Jowell J, Thomas JC, van Zyl Smit J (eds) Rule of law symposium 2014: the importance of rule of law in promoting development. Singapore Academy of Law and Bingham Centre for the Rule of Law, Singapore, pp 81–102

Schill SW, Vidigal G (2018) Cutting the Gordian Knot: investment dispute settlement à la Carte, RTA exchange. Geneva International Centre for Trade and Sustainable Development and the Inter-America Development Bank, Geneva

Schmid M (2013) Switzerland. In: Brown C (ed) Commentaries on selected model investment treaties. Oxford University Press, Oxford, pp 651–696

Schreuer CH (2004) Travelling the BIT route: of waiting periods, Umbrella Clauses and Forks in the Road. J World Invest Trade 5(2):231–256

Schreuer CH (2005) Calvo's grandchild: the return of local remedies in investment arbitration. Law Practice Int Courts Tribunals 4(1):1–17

Schreuer CH (2006) Diversity and harmonization of treaty interpretation in investment arbitration. Transnational Dispute Manag 3(2):1

Schreuer CH (2008) Preliminary rulings in investment arbitration. In: Sauvant K (ed) Appeals mechanism in international investment disputes. Oxford University Press, Oxford, pp 207–212

Schreuer CH (2010) Interaction of international tribunals and domestic courts in investment law. Contemp Iss Int Arbitr Mediation Fordham Papers 4:71–94

Schreuer CH, Malintoppi L, Reinisch A, Sinclair A (2009) The ICSID Convention—a commentary, 2nd edn. Cambridge University Press, Cambridge

Schultz T, Dupont C (2015) Investment arbitration: promoting the rule of law or over-empowering investors? A quantitative empirical study. Eur J Int Law 25(4):1147–1168

Shany Y (2007) Regulating jurisdictional relations between national and international courts. Oxford University Press, Oxford

Shihata IFI (1986) Towards a greater de-politicisation of investment disputes: the roles of ICSID and MIGA. ICSID Rev Foreign Invest Law J 1(1):1–32

Siegmann T (2007) The impact of bilateral investment treaties and double taxation treaties on foreign direct investments, University of St. Gallen Law School Law and Economics Research Paper Series, Working Paper No. 2008-22 (November 2007)

Sornarajah M (2010) The international law on foreign investment. Cambridge University Press, Cambridge

Spiermann O (2009) Premature treaty claims. In: Binder C, Kriebaum U, Reinisch A, Wittich S (eds) International investment law for the 21st century. Oxford University Press, Oxford, pp 463–489

Stigen J (2008) The relationship between the international criminal court and national jurisdictions: the principle of complementarity. Brill|Nijhoff, Leiden

Swenson DL (2005) Why do developing countries sign bilateral investment treaties? U.C. Davis J Int Law Policy 12:131–155

Tietje C, Baetens F (2014) The impact of investor-state-dispute settlement (ISDS) in the transatlantic trade and investment partnership, Study prepared for the Minister for Foreign Trade and Development Cooperation and the Ministry of Foreign Affairs of the Netherlands

Tobin J, Rose-Ackerman S (2005) Foreign direct investment and the business environment in developing countries: the impact of bilateral investment treaties, Yale Law and Economics Research Paper No. 293, 2 May 2005, pp 1–52

Tobin J, Rose-Ackerman S (2006) Bilateral investment treaties: do they stimulate foreign direct investment? Yale University Law School e-publications, New Haven, pp 1–42

Tortian A (2012) The impact of bilateral investment treaties and financial development on foreign direct investment: evidence from Eurasia. In: Paper submission for the Armenian economic association conference, Haigazian University, Yerevan, Armenia (13–14 October 2012)

Trackman L (2012) Choosing domestic courts over investor–state arbitration: Australia's repudiation of the status Quo. UNSW Law J 35(3):979–1012

van den Berg AJ (2019) Appeal mechanisms for ISDS awards: interaction with New York and ICISD Conventions. In: Asian Academy of International Law's proceedings ISDS reform conference 2019, mapping the way forward, Hong Kong SAR, China, (13 February 2019)

Van Harten G (2010) Five justifications for investment treaties: a critical discussion. Trade Law Dev 2(1):19–58

Vandevelde KJ (1988) Reassessing the Hickenlooper amendment. Va J Int Law 29(1):115–168

Vandevelde K (1998) Investment liberalization and economic development: the role of bilateral investment treaties. Columbia J Transnational Law 36:501–527

Vandevelde KJ (2009) U.S. international investment agreements. Oxford University Press, Oxford

Vidigal G, Stevens B (2018) Brazil's new model of dispute settlement for investment: return to the past or alternative for the future? J World Invest Trade 19:475–512

Virzo R (2011) The preliminary ruling procedures at international regional courts and tribunals. Law Practice Int Courts Tribunals 10(2):285–313

Vis-Dunbar D, Nikiema HS (30 April 2009) Do bilateral investment treaties lead to more foreign investment? Investment Treaty News. Available at https://www.iisd.org/itn/2009/04/30/do-bilateral-investment-treaties-lead-to-more-foreign-investment/

Wegen G, Markert L (2010) Food for thought on fork-in-the-road — a clause awakens from its hibernation. In: Zeiler G, Welser I et al (eds) Austrian yearbook on international arbitration, vol 2010. MANZ Verlag, Vienna, pp 269–292

Yackee JW (2006) Sacrificing sovereignty: bilateral investment treaties, international arbitration, and the quest for capital' USC CLEO Research Paper No. C06-15, pp 2–92

Yackee JW (2007) Do BITs really work? Revisiting the empirical link between investment treaties and foreign direct investment, legal studies research paper series (University of Wisconsin Law School), Paper No. 1054 (October 2007)

Yackee JW (2008) Bilateral investment treaties, credible commitment, and the rule of (international) law: do BITs promote foreign direct investment? Law Soc Rev 42:805–832

The manufacturer's authorised representative in the EU is Springer Nature Customer Service Centre GmbH, Europaplatz 3, 69115 Heidelberg, Germany. If you have any concerns regarding our products, please contact ProductSafety@springernature.com

Printed and bound by CPI Group (UK) Ltd, Croydon, CR0 4YY
05/10/2026
02228155-0006